Praise for *Notes to Scr*

"... turns the thankless task of rewriting into a process of discovery and an experience of revelation. Notes tell you a reader found a problem. Barbara and Vicki tell you how to know what that problem really is."
— CHARLES SLOCUM, Assistant Executive Director, Writers Guild of America, West

"On the short list of *must-reads* for every film and TV writer.... Strongly recommended for those whose job it is to give notes. If both sides of the table had this book in their hands, the world would be a happier place."
— DENA HIGLEY, Emmy Award–winning head writer, *Days of Our Lives, One Life to Live*; author, *Momaholic*

"I LOVED this book! It plainly and succinctly explains things it took me fifteen years in Hollywood to learn. It tells a writer exactly what to expect from notes, and exactly how to respond — which will save them a world of pain."
— KAREN HALL, writer and producer, *Judging Amy, Moonlighting, M*A*S*H*

"The road to obsolescence is paved with writers who never learned how to receive, interpret, and execute notes. The authors give young scribes the tools to tackle this hugely important but ever-neglected part of the job."
— SCOTT TEEMS, screenwriter, *That Evening Sun, Rectify*

"A gift.... Provides that long-needed bridge between the too-oft-times warring factions: the misunderstood writer versus the equally misunderstood executive, producer, agent, publisher.... Helps the writer create the best work possible.... Lifts the veil on the confusions, standoffs, and utter frustration that can be the creative process."
— BOBETTE BUSTER, story consultant, Pixar, FOX; Adjunct Professor, USC School of Cinema

"... tells it like it is for screenwriters, offering straightforward and practical insider advice on how to write a good script and how to survive and flourish in this tough and crazy business.... The perfect guide to maneuvering through the often tricky and murky waters of launching and sustaining a successful writing career."
— BUZZ MCLAUGHLIN, author, *The Playwright's Process*; Program Director for the New Hampshire Institute of Art, MFA in Writing for Stage and Screen

"Reading this book may take away your last excuse not to write and / or rewrite your beloved screenplay.... Insightful.... A book on how to write a great script, not just how to survive our industry. I'm keeping this one by my keyboard."
— CLARE SERA, screenwriter, *Blended*

"Where was this book 20 years ago when I was starting out? It will save much pain, turmoil, and time for those who read it and learn.... A gift to writers and those who work with writers. The Rules for Professional Screenwriters alone is worth the price of the book."
— JOAN CONSIDINE JOHNSON, writer / producer, *Sue Thomas: F.B.Eye, Doc, Olivia, Rugrats*

"Every pro screenwriter I've ever met has the same few dog-eared screenwriting-fundamentals books on their shelves. To those writers, these books are more precious than gold. *Notes* is about to take up residence in writing offices across Hollywood. An instant classic. If you're looking to break in, this needs to be in your collection."
— BRIAN BIRD, writer / producer, *When Calls the Heart, Touched by an Angel*

"A 'must-read' for aspiring writers as well as practitioners.... Penned with wisdom and wit.... Brilliant.... Peppered with examples of what works and what doesn't, all offered with insight and humor. Should be required reading in all screenwriting courses."
— Patricia F. Phalen, PhD, Associate Professor, School of Media and Public Affairs, The George Washington University

"The note I give the most often as a development executive is the one I find most frustrating as a writer: 'I'm not engaged with your characters or what's happening.' Barbara and Vicki offer a much-needed strategy to answer this note, and about a thousand others.... They dig into the guts of what makes a story, and what makes a story work."
— John Burd, Manager, Production & Development, MarVista Entertainment

"Creative and unique.... Translates cryptic phrases like 'It's not edgy enough' and 'Where's the sizzle?' into actionable ideas.... An exciting launching pad for examining what works in your script, and also a way to gauge what readers and buyers might actually be taking away from the material."
— Ron Fernandez, Director, MFA Film and Television, Mount St. Mary's College

"A fresh approach for new writers who think they've heard it all.... A solid perspective on writing that sheds new light on how to take feedback and make a script better. A must-read."
— Steve McEveety, producer, *What Women Want, Braveheart*

"... contains fantastic exercises designed to help you develop your characters, your plot, your theme, your whole damn script. I'm working on a project right now, and literally turned to this to get over humps in my character development."
— Chad Gervich, writer / producer, *Wipeout, After Lately, Dog With a Blog*

"A great buffer to help soften potential blows to your ego and your skills as a writer. The book goes beyond the basics of just notes and gives both beginners and veterans something to help their writing process."
— Matthew Terry, screenwriter / filmmaker / teacher

"... takes away the dread of receiving notes and provides constructive and realistic [solutions] that are applicable to any screenplay, giving the writer the opportunity to solve most issues.... One of the most useful tools in a screenwriter's toolbox."
— Stefan Blitz, Editor-in-Chief, *Forces of Geek*

"All the elements for a screenwriting and writing companion. Eye-opening for connecting your script with audiences, and making the cinematic experience compelling."
— Dave Watson, editor, *Movies Matter*

"... treats the storyteller as someone with a noble calling who can always strive to be better. Drawing from their vast experience in the film industry, the authors reveal solid strategies for utilizing feedback to shape a story into its best possible form. Screenwriters at any level of experience will benefit from this book."
— Tom Farr, writer

"A wealth of information. *All* screenwriters will learn to create better and more compelling stories. Read this book only if your skin is thick enough to handle the truth about what you put into your screenplays."
— Forris Day Jr., writer / reviewer, *Scared Stiff Reviews*, ScriptMag.com

Notes

TO SCREENWRITERS

Advancing Your Story, Screenplay, and Career with
WHATEVER HOLLYWOOD THROWS AT YOU

BARBARA NICOLOSI AND VICKI PETERSON

MICHAEL WIESE PRODUCTIONS

Published by Michael Wiese Productions
12400 Ventura Blvd. #1111
Studio City, CA 91604
(818) 379-8799, (818) 986-3408 (FAX)
mw@mwp.com
www.mwp.com

Cover design by Johnny Ink. www.johnnyink.com
Interior design by William Morosi
Printed by McNaughton & Gunn

Manufactured in the United States of America

Library of Congress Cataloging-in-Publication Data

Nicolosi, Barbara R.
 Notes to Screenwriters: Advancing Your Story, Screenplay, and Career With Whatever Hollywood Throws at You / Barbara R. Nicolosi and Vicki Peterson; foreword by David McFadzean.
    pages cm
 Includes bibliographical references.
 ISBN 978-1-61593-213-9
1. Motion picture authorship. 2. Motion picture authorship--Marketing. I. Peterson, Vicki II. Title.
PN1996.N53 2015
808.2'3--dc23

                              2014018798

Printed on Recycled Stock

CONTENTS

Section III: THE WORKING SCREENWRITER 139

For Delle Chatman

1951–2006

"A screenplay is a work of art."

ACKNOWLEDGMENTS

Vicki: Aside from being the love of my life, my husband Tim is my biggest supporter, a wonderful encourager, and the reason why I get to do what I love to do. Thank you, sweetheart, for tending to real matters of life and death at your job so I can tend to imaginary ones in mine. To my three beautiful children, Zanna, Lucy, and Timothy: You will always be my greatest productions, of whom I am most proud. You inspire me to make the most of life. Thank you to my whole cheering section of family and friends: I am grateful for your patience with me when I disappear under a deadline. Your prayers keep me going. Special thanks to my Act One mentors, and my professor, Buzz McLaughlin, for your optimism and love of artists.

Barbara: Everything I am and have ever done is because of the love, support, and formation I received from my family. Thanks, Mom and Dad, for insisting that we read lots of books; for pushing us to be discerning as regards media; and for systematically exposing us to beauty through the arts. Thanks to my sister, Alison, for always believing in me; and to Valerie for being an artistic perfectionist; and to Cynthia for critiquing my very first screenplay with the blasé note, "You can do better." I also thank my loving husband, Norris, for his belief and support, and for being so lovely about all the nights I didn't have dinner ready because we were working on the book. My primary influences as a thinker are traceable back to my philosophy professor, Dr. John Barger, who passed on his indelible conviction that philosophy was a gritty, necessary component of "a life worth living." My love for cinema as an art form is directly due to the influence of my screenwriting professor at Northwestern, the late and greatly missed Delle Chatman. Do they read in Heaven, Delle? If so, I hope you are pleased. Finally, thanks to Dr. David Weeks at Azusa Pacific University for getting me and my Aristotle thing.

From both of us: We also thank the many Hollywood friends and mentors who have been so generous with their insight, counsel, and encouragement. We mean you, Ron Austin, David McFadzean, Karen and Jim Covell, Chris Riley, Chuck Slocum, Dick Lyles, Clare Sera, Father Willy Raymond, Father Don Woznicki, Karen Hall, Nancy Miller, Chuck Konzelman, Cary Solomon, Bobette Buster, Scott and T. J. Teems, and all of our friends and colleagues at Act One. Thanks to our essential and sadly missed collaborators David Schall, Jack Gilbert, and Ava Memmen. Thanks to Chip MacGregor and everyone at MacGregor Literary; and to Joel Cheek, our amazing graphic designer.

A special acknowledgment to the screenwriters whose work we quote herein: Robert Bolt, Raymond Chandler, Francis Ford Coppola, Michael Crichton, Cameron Crowe, Nora Ephron, Julius J. Epstein, Philip G. Epstein, Brian Helgeland, Sidney Howard, Howard Koch, David Koepp, David Mamet, Edmund H. North, Aaron Sorkin, Donald Ogden Stewart, Jeb Stuart, David Twohy, and Billy Wilder.

Finally, we owe this book to all the students and writers with whom we've worked over the last twenty years. To everyone who has given us good story notes, thank you for making our projects better. To everyone who has given us bad story notes, thank you for making us better as writers! Thanks to all the students and writers who have shared their work with us as we have struggled to unlock the secrets of story with you and for you. This book is for you.

HOW TO USE THIS BOOK

If you are a writer but have never written a screenplay...
Skip to Chapter 3 and read through Chapter 16. These chapters cover the essential elements of a screenplay, and basic technical information about standard industry formatting. Use each of the chapters and the accompanying exercises to guide you as you flesh out another part of your project — from the story and plot to the characters, arena, structure, dialogue, and cinematic quality. When you start writing pages, refer to the section on formatting to ensure that what you write looks like a real screenplay. After you finish a draft, move to Section III for what to do next.

If you are a writer who has written one or more screenplays, but has never gotten them read or considered anywhere...
Begin at Section III and read the chapters about the business. Before you do your rewrite, move back in the book to Section I.

If you are a screenwriter who is getting feedback from professors, writing groups, producers, or story consultants...
This book is really for you. Take a few minutes before diving in to make a list of the general notes that you are getting on your project. Put the notes in categories like "Notes on Me as the Writer," or "Notes on My Screenplay Story," or "Notes on My Technical Style." Make your way through the whole book from the beginning, completing all the content exercises. When you find one of the notes on your list in the heading of a chapter, you know where to start working. Read that chapter and work it against your screenplay.

If you are a producer, development executive, educator, or investor...
Start by reading the first section of the book, on the notes experience for writers. Try and put yourself in the shoes of the writers

on the other side of your desk. Then move through the rest of the book, paying particular attention to the chapters headed by notes you give all too often. Maybe it's time to find a new way to talk about these same old problems.

If you are just somebody who really just wants to grow in love and appreciation of visual storytelling...

You should focus on the heart of the book, from Chapter 3 to Chapter 12. We're breaking open the stuff of great stories and movies for you in a way that we hope will revitalize the way you watch the screen art forms. We guarantee, at some point, you'll find you're suddenly a real crackerjack about movies!

FOREWORD

After working with hundreds of writers, directors, and producers, it's clear that creative passion is the fuel that drives the best of them. But it's also clear that a project rarely succeeds on passion alone. It is essential, but it is not the "be-all and end-all." If a writer, director, or producer doesn't know how to effectively listen to feedback, or doesn't have a firm grasp of dramatic form, the result is almost always disaster.

Let me give you an example. Many years ago, a producer friend of mine was working on a film that ran into problems with the studio. The studio executives sent the producer to tell the director that his cut of the film was poorly structured and not funny enough for a mainstream audience.

What was the director's response? He told the studio that he wasn't going to make any of their suggested changes. Why? Because he didn't make the film for a mainstream audience; this was "a comedy for smart people." You can imagine how well that went over with the studio execs.

Angry phone calls flew back and forth. Lawyers got involved. Lawsuits were threatened. Actors began to speak publically about how the studio was "stealing" the film. It was a gigantic mess. Finally, after weeks of bickering, the studio gave up. The film was finished and made ready for testing.

For those who aren't familiar with the testing process, here it is in a nutshell: A recruited audience of 300 or more watches the film. Afterward, each participant fills out a questionnaire that grades the film. 100 is perfect; 0 is a disaster. Most films score somewhere between 60 and 80. Hit films score 90 and above.

The studio set up the test screening and let the director pick the theater. He picked a theater in one of the wealthiest zip codes in America, one where "smart people lived." (It also happened to be his home turf.)

At the end of the screening, an executive from the company that did the testing approached the director with the results. The company executive was flabbergasted. He'd been doing film testing for 25 years, and this was the lowest test score he'd ever seen! You would think this might rattle the director's confidence, at least a bit. But what was his response? "I think the critics will like it."

It turns out that the testing was right, and the director was wrong. The film had a budget of $17 million (midrange in those years) and earned a mere $245,000 at the box office. A complete loss for the studio.

It was out of theaters within a matter of days. I guess there just weren't enough smart people. And what was the critics' response? On Rotten Tomatoes, the movie got a 17% "fresh" rating. Which of course means that 83% of the critics were also not smart people.

There are at least two lessons in this story. The director had gotten feedback that his film had problems. This feedback came from many knowledgeable people, and at least deserved some consideration. But he couldn't hear it. You know the adage: If you're at a party, and one person tells you you're drunk, you can probably ignore him. But if ten people tell you you're drunk, you should probably listen. The director was drunk. With creative passion.

Secondly, the film had some very obvious structural issues that the producer had pointed out several times. And what was the director's excuse for having not addressed them? He was breaking new ground. He referred the producer to a Picasso quote: "Learn the rules like a pro so you can break them like an artist." Smart people love quotes. The producer replied that there was a reason why after more than 2,000 years, Aristotle's *Poetics* was still the basis for every screenwriting book in print. (That comment got the producer booted out of the edit bay.)

I wish I could say that this story is unique. It isn't. If you talk to people in the business, you will hear similar stories repeated ad nauseam. How many times have I heard a writer or director reel off Picasso's quote, only to discover they don't know the very rules that they are breaking?

That's where Barbara and Vicki's book, *Notes to Screenwriters*, becomes an invaluable tool. It's a delightful and insightful short course in screenwriting. Easy reading with thoughtful, stimulating content. It works on all levels, whether you've written a dozen scripts or none. It can be a refresher or a primer.

On reading *Notes to Screenwriters*, I was reminded of many things I had known but lost over the years, and I learned some interesting new things that hadn't occurred to me. It is a welcome and fresh new resource for all screenwriters.

DAVID MCFADZEAN
Executive Producer,
What Women Want,
Home Improvement

INTRODUCTION
THE BOOK THAT NOTES BUILT

> *A writer is someone for whom writing is more*
> *difficult than it is for other people.*
> — THOMAS MANN

When a work of art is good, that's partly because it's unique. It's part of art's goodness that it feels creative, crisp, different. This is particularly true in storytelling. When a story feels new and different, it's a sign it is working well.

When stories fail, they tend to do so for all the same reasons, which make them feel *beginnerish*, derivative, and hackneyed. But getting a visual story to the ecstasy of "new" is a kind of agony for the writer. The task is complicated: The only sure way to make something feel really fresh and new is to use classical storytelling techniques that have been set in stone for thousands of years. It's only by skillfully reaching backward that a writer can move his or her story forward. This is because story has a nature and a form that must be adhered to, or the thing created will not be a story. The challenge is to make something new using the existing form.

"Notes" is the word Hollywood uses to address problems in a script or project idea. Everybody who reads your script will give you notes. There are even names for the kinds of notes that people can give you on your project. There are "overall notes" for broad problems in the project. There are "line notes" for questions about word usage in dialogue and description. There are "format notes" for technical problems in the screenplay style. And then there are "story notes," "character notes," "structure notes," and "business notes." In short, there are lots and lots of ways for the myriad people in the business to find fault with your screenplay.

The sad thing is that many of the notes people give on projects are completely useless. That's partly because, along with the hackneyed stories, the notes themselves have become clichéd. Integrity prohibits it, but it would be possible to hand the same set of notes off on script after script. It's rare to find a script that has a new problem.

Another reason notes don't offer much help is that the people giving them often don't know any better than the writer what the true problem with the script is. Even if they have the correct instincts, they still may not have the vocabulary of story to help the writer pinpoint the project's flaws — and allow their repair without the destruction of the components that are working well.

There are lots of examples of useless notes that get given over and over again to sincerely striving or hapless writers: "I didn't care about your characters." "I wasn't engaged in the reading, and found it a slog." "I never understood why you were telling *this* story." "There was too much going on." "There wasn't enough going on." "It needs a hook."

Notes to Screenwriters is the synthesis of our attempt to always give better, more helpful notes to writers and producers. We've tried to get to the bottom of the clichéd notes, and ascertain the real causes behind why we don't care and why the read is a slog and why the story just doesn't seem to cohere. Chances are, if a production company passes on your script, it's because of one or more of the "little gems" we've collected for you here.

The second part of the book is spent breaking down the rules of screenplay format. This kind of problem forms the bulk of so many "line notes" because mistakes in format mess with the whole way a screenplay should work as a technical document. If a project doesn't work technically, it isn't going to get a chance to work any other way — so buckle down and get your formatting act together.

Finally, the last part of the book is all the best tips we have heard and shared about living a successful life as a professional writer in the entertainment industry. The sad truth is, lots of good projects go nowhere because the writer has no *savoir faire* about finding and working with collaborators. In the end, people will prefer to work with a bad project more than with an unprofessional writer. A bad project can be fixed, but taking on a difficult writer who is clueless about the business is a thankless task.

This book is not meant to be a complete "how to" of screenwriting. It isn't meant to analyze types of characters. It isn't meant to provide a foundation in the wonderful and terrible craft of screenwriting. This book presumes you are already somewhat schooled in storytelling, and particularly in screen storytelling.

This book is built upon the detailed mentoring we've given to clients. Some of the material requires taking in a deeper vision of the meaning and purpose of story. Some of the material consists of bullet points and lists of things to consider.

You are being put in a development executive's office to determine why you or your story idea or your screenplay isn't working. Our intention is to break standard industry notes down into the reasons behind them. Why is it that you don't care about my characters? What is it that makes my dialogue flat? Why does my project feel like it is meandering and in search of a point? Why don't people like to work with me? We're trying to best articulate the notes that the executive might give. And we're offering you, the writer, some practical, pithy, and hopefully insightful suggestions on how to address those notes.

SECTION I
BROAD NOTES

CHAPTER 1

NOTES ON TAKING NOTES

THE NOTES (FROM A WRITER'S POV):

- "So, after all that, did they like it?"
- "Didn't they see that great metaphor I put in there?"
- "I can't believe they didn't pick up on my theme."
- "Why does she keep repeating that? I don't understand it!"
- "Did they even read it?"
- "They think I'm a hack. I know they think I'm a hack."

THE NOTES (FROM A PRODUCER'S POV):

- "Why is she getting so upset? This is embarrassing."
- "He can't even seem to hear what I'm saying."
- "Do I need to be here for this?"
- "I don't need to know *why* you wrote what you wrote. I need you to accept that it's not working."
- "I don't care how hard it is to fix this problem. That's your job."

For writers, getting notes can be a terrifying, anxiety-ridden, and depressing experience. You've spent months, if not years, putting everything you have into your script, agonizing over every transition and slugline. Your themes matter deeply to you, and often come from your own personal struggles and failures. There is a little bit (or a lot) of your own heart and soul in each of your characters. So now you have to turn over the baby you've birthed and nurtured to a bunch of people who will spend a fraction as much time, effort, and soul sweat as you have on it, and then hope that it will be enjoyed and appreciated. And it usually isn't. Your precious project is set on the altar of show business, awaiting sacrifice.

When we give script consultations, invariably we notice the writer's sweaty palms and the tremor in their voices. Or else, there is just way too much bravado, which generally is masking lots of hurt and insecurity. Often, when we're giving notes, the first five to ten minutes is about getting writers to *just calm down* so that they can hear us and hopefully trust us.

We understand. We're writers, too, and we've been on the other end of that table. We've gotten some of the most debilitating, humiliating, unhelpful notes ever. Want proof?

> *Barbara: One time a producer gave a note that she didn't understand a certain line in my script. When I coughed that it was supposed to be a joke, her voice got really disgusted. "Well, it isn't funny. Get rid of it. And you know what? You aren't funny. So why don't you go through the whole script and take out everything you think is funny to just save me time?"*
>
> *Vicki: There was the producer who one week told me she loved my script, thought it was flawless. Then the next week, she called to tell me it was terrible and that nothing was working. I hadn't changed anything. The next several weeks I endured the same pattern of whiplash-inducing notes!*
>
> *Barbara: Or the time I had a script optioned by a team of two producers who happened to be husband and wife. They liked to read their scripts one at a time, and have each give their own set of notes. So the wife read my project first and gave seventeen story notes. Not wanting to be difficult, I made the changes she had requested. Then the husband read the script and gave twenty of his own notes. And about fourteen of his notes requested I reverse the changes I had made for his wife! What to do?*
>
> *Vicki: Or then there was the jealous cowriter who tried to boot me off a project by telling our producers that I wasn't a "real" writer and she*

couldn't work with me. The producers called her bluff, but those were some long days sitting in the room together working on the project — which, to no one's surprise, fell apart.

We could go on. Together, we've had producers pick up coverage notes from their interns (not having read the script themselves) as they're walking into the room to tell us what's wrong with our story. We've seen investors nitpick arbitrary details and ignore major storylines. We've had to go into notes meetings and explain to wanna-be "players" what a turning point is.

We get it.

But we've also been on the other side of the table as producers giving notes.

We've tried and tried to get a writer to make a change that everybody in a hundred miles knew needed to be made, only to have the writer shrug: "That's not my vision." We've had a writer break into a defensive sneer: "Well, *my* stories don't have endings!" We've had students sniff that Aristotle wasn't as smart as some people say. We've seen writers insist that they have tried every possible way to fix a problem and it just can't be fixed, so we should just accept it. We've seen crying and emotional breakdowns, and desperate spontaneous therapy sessions all because some writers just didn't know how to take notes.

One word, writers: Relax.

Getting notes doesn't have to be quite so scary. In fact, it can be quite exciting and affirming — even when the script isn't working. After all, a notes session means someone has *at last* been reading your work. Someone else wants to hear about the characters and situations with whom you've been alone for months or years. And then there is the chance you'll find the rare treat of a reader or producer who really values your work, and is eager to meet you because of it.

When a writer knows how to properly decipher notes, it can be a liberating experience. A writer wields power. You are the creator of your story, and have the opportunity to make the work the very best it can be. You are literally the hero of your own stories. You just have to realize it.

So why all the terror? Because even in surprisingly famous places with people getting paid big bucks, the notes that are flying around can be cryptic and confusing. Lots of folks who are working as junior development execs or company "gateways" have law degrees or business degrees but are otherwise completely unprepared to analyze a screenplay. Lots of script buyers are only set up to say "no" and have no interest in communicating why it's a no, so dealing with them feels like a series of mystifying and brutal slamming doors. Lots of other folks giving notes have agendas coloring their comments that are unbeknownst to the writer; for instance, the famous, "We want this to be more something we can give to our fifty-eight-year-old actress friend, so we need to lose all the skateboarding stuff." Finally, receiving criticism is always hard. No matter how mature you are, it hurts when someone tells you your characters aren't interesting, your theme is kind of lame, your imagery isn't working.

It's too much to ask writers to embrace the pitfalls and suffering of the notes process, but we do have one golden rule that everyone in the storytelling arena needs to hear:

Learn from everything.

The notes phase is bracing, but because it is necessary, a professional writer has to learn to cope with and benefit from the process. The good news is, notes from people who read a lot of scripts generally hold some truth to them, no matter how poorly constructed they are. It is the job of the writer to interpret the notes and then apply the right fixes. A writer who is determined to make a notes session part of his ongoing professional development rarely falls prey to the emotional and psychological pitfalls therein.

Here are some guidelines to maximize the experience of getting notes:

- **Keep the main thing the main thing.** A notes session is not about you. It's about the project. Don't waste the note-giver's time trying to explain or make excuses for your script.

Don't expect to be praised and affirmed. Don't come in looking to make a friend. The point of the encounter is to fix the problems with your project.

- **Don't make it personal.** Even if it is. Don't focus on the reasons the note-giver might have to want to hurt you or get you to quit or ruin your screenplay. Never respond to a script or story note with a personal comment about the note-giver. That the note-giver might be being unprofessional doesn't give you license to lose your dignity too.

- **Figure out the note-giver's story language.** Everyone has a different way of talking about movies and stories. Everyone has a different scale for what makes a movie good and what is a lesser problem. It's a very good idea to get notes from a range of people for this reason: Every new person will give you feedback on the aspect of movies that is most important to them, and all of the aspects are important in the end. If a note-giver says, "That scene really worked," it is up to the writer to find out what they mean and exactly how it worked. When you say "worked," do you mean it was emotionally satisfying? Was it a clever and surprising payoff or reversal? Was it a moment of psychological revelation or artistic adeptness? The writer has to place themselves into the mind and mode out of which the note-giver speaks. It isn't up to the writer to give the note-writer a lesson in screenwriting jargon. You need to be an interpreter.

- **Keep it positive.** Even if you're terrified, cling to the good news. While many note sessions are focused on what's "wrong" with a story, absorb what's right about the story, too. If your note-giver doesn't tell you what's to like in your project, ask.

- **Believe there are few "bad" notes.** Some notes are more helpful than others, but all notes are an opportunity to improve. Your willingness to grow and improve as a writer is what will set you apart and make you succeed in the long run, so consider every opportunity a gift.

- **When you do get a bad note**, nod thoughtfully, write it down, and imagine with which friend you can most enjoy laughing about it later. With a beer. Never snap back, be sarcastic, or get defensive.

- **Trust your note-giver.** We know it's hard to do this sometimes, but if you truly believe that the person has your best interests at heart and really wants to help you tell a great story, the way you take notes will dramatically improve.

- **Don't give up your babies too soon.** Some writers are so desperate to not appear difficult that they never explain or defend the choices they made in their scripts. Remember, the person giving the notes has probably only read the script once or twice, while you, the writer, have brooded over every comma for months or years. No one knows the script as well as you. Some insights are worth fighting for, or at least defending in a non-argumentative way.

- **Clarify, clarify, clarify.** Adopt phrases like, "So, what I'm hearing is..." Even if you think you understand a note, restate it in your own words. Misunderstandings lead to lots of wasted time rewriting things in the wrong way.

- **Ask questions.** It's easy for writers to get defensive, which is one step away from shutting down. If you find yourself doing this, try asking more questions. This will help you direct your energies toward a more positive solution.

- **Thank your note-giver.** Always. Even if you didn't think the notes were helpful, treat your note-giver with respect.

- **Give yourself a treat.** No, really, don't skip this. After a notes session, plan a small reward for yourself. Go watch a movie with a friend, or get some ice cream; whatever you want. It makes a huge difference when you're in a meeting and you know you have something to look forward to afterward. Try it, and see if you don't leave your meeting more upbeat.

CHAPTER 2

NOTES ON THE STORYTELLER

The Notes:

- **"I don't think this writer can 'go there.'"**
- **"This project needs someone steeped in Eskimo culture."**
- **"This writer just isn't funny / dramatic / weird enough to be writing this."**
- **"There needs to be a lot more depth in a topic like this."**
- **"The writer needs more life experience."**

Some writers are just wrong for some stories. Much of our script and story consulting work comes down to problems caused by writers working on projects that are too advanced for them, or completely outside their voice. Generally, people who want to write movies go out and buy Final Draft software and a couple of books and then start typing away. It's worse than someone just buying paint and a canvas and starting to paint. It's like someone with no training buying drafting paper and starting to design a skyscraper. Nobody wants to ride in *that* elevator.

Part of professionalism in a writer is to assess in each project whether one has the skill set, voice / style, depth, and courage to handle a story. But let's face it: Most writers are burning to write something — anything — that has the potential to go somewhere. Here are some ways to know whether you should option that book, or take that job.

a. Are You Good Enough?

Generally, a beginning writer comes to the craft with a passion project glimmering in his or her imagination. The writer has already written an Academy Award acceptance speech for the project, even though it's mainly just a few story moments in his head. Almost universally, the high passion project is not the one to use as a writer's first or second spec script. Most newbies are just not good enough to do their own passion project justice.

This is not to say that we should only work on projects that are easy for us. Every script should see a writer advancing in his skills. Screenwriting is a highly detailed, complex, and layered art form, and everybody's first efforts are bad. Having a bad first effort doesn't mean you are a bad screenwriter. It just means you are doing it. Your writing will improve the more you do it. This is a profession founded on perseverance. As a wise man once said, "You can't lose 'em all." If you have any talent at all, and keep producing proposals and drafts, and keep expanding your network of contacts, and take opportunities when they come, eventually you will see your work forge ahead.

Having said that, there are levels of expertise in screenwriting, as in any art form. Be careful of hubris that would have you take on a project that will demand more of you than you have to give. It isn't just about you. Taking money for a job that you aren't good enough to write reflects a lack of integrity. Sometimes the project is going to require the integration of more conflicts than you can handle. Sometimes it's going to require a level of research that is beyond your possibilities. Sometimes it's going to require bolder cinematic techniques than you can deliver. Sometimes it's going to be in a genre for which your voice and style are unsuited.

It's good to accept projects that will stretch you. It's bad to accept projects that will break you. It's demoralizing to leave something incomplete or to be replaced because you just couldn't deliver.

It's very discouraging to fail at something, so be careful not to set yourself up for failure.

So, how do you know whether you are good enough to take on a particular project? Think of it in the same way a runner knows if they are ready for a marathon. That is, they start with a mile run on roads. They get really good. Then, they try running in hills. They decide roads are a better fit. They add another mile. Then, they start meeting with pros and stocking up on gear. They get better. One day, they enter into a 5K race. They do badly but have some fun, so they hire a coach. Soon, they are running lots of events, some longer than 5K. They do better each time, and really start to enjoy all the aspects of competition. Before they know it, somebody tells them they should enter a marathon, and there they are.

Screenwriting is the marathon of the writing life. Beginners should start with reading screenplays. A lot of them. As many as possible. Especially the good ones, which have won awards and stood the test of time.

"Now am I ready to write a feature screenplay?"

No.

Now, you should read craft-oriented books to help you understand what you've seen in the screenplays. Classes on screenwriting are useful as well, of course.

Your goal in all this research and study is to identify the essential skill sets required for the screenwriting art form. You need to name the skills, have an always greater understanding of the nature of those skills, and then begin to master them. Some will come easier to you than others. Build on your strengths, but you can't ignore the skills at which you are weak, especially if they are essential skills. You have to minimally become competent in the essentials the way a long-distance runner can't neglect his stride or breathing technique or other muscle training.

As in running, good coaching is key. There are many screenwriting "gurus" out there, and many of them are saying the same thing in their own way. Find the one who speaks best to you. Your goal is to learn the universals of the craft. If there's a particular technique you like, study it until you've mastered it, and test it against new information from other sources.

"*Now* am I ready to write a feature screenplay?"

Probably not. Get back to us after you've turned out a couple of short scripts.

b. Can You "Go There"?

> *The writer, when he is also an artist,*
> *is someone who admits what others do not dare reveal.*
> — ELIA KAZAN

There's an exercise we have used very successfully in our work with new screenwriters that is derived from the book *The Elements of Playwriting* by the late Dr. Louis Catron. Dr. Catron's insight was that until a writer had composed a personal credo, his or her work would feel flat, derivative, and cheap. Moreover, without a credo, most people would walk away from their dream of being a professional writer as soon as they realized how many considerably easier ways to make a living there were.

The word "credo" means "I believe" in Latin, and it comes from the list of Christian beliefs as found in the ancient Nicene Creed. Everyone has a credo, even if they haven't ever written one down or put it into words. Our deepest convictions are flinging us into all the choices of our lives, even though we may never stop to think why we do what we do. A credo is another word for a person's hierarchy of moral values, the way they determine good from evil, and their understanding of how human beings should dwell together. Chuck Slocum, who served for years as the strategic director of the Writers Guild of America, is fond of saying, "Every screenplay is a work of theology. Even if the writer doesn't believe in God."

Writers do not have the luxury of an unconscious credo. They need to bring to the fore all their most deeply held convictions, because their point of view is half of what they have to sell. The other half is how they communicate what they believe. We always recommend that writers set aside some time to ask themselves: "What do I really believe?" "What do I really know to be true?" and then write the answers down as a series of affirmative statements like this:

- "I believe that in the end the truth always comes out."
- "I believe that while they have life, human beings have value because they are always vessels of love pouring in and flowing out."
- "I believe that we can't carry the people we love, that we can only move obstacles out of their way."
- "I believe that no one can have a more deeply vested interested in one's life than oneself."
- "I believe that suffering makes human beings deeper."

The usefulness of writing out a credo is to help a writer figure out exactly what they bring to the table regarding recurring themes. If you've done this, you will have a pretty good sense when a project comes your way if it is appropriate for you thematically. If the project isn't you, you can try and make it something you can do. But if the material can't be stretched that way, you'd better pass.

We once worked with a writer who had very strong views about feminism and patriarchy. The producer who had hired her called us because the writer just couldn't abandon her strident views to write the lighthearted romantic comedy that was on the agenda. We met with her and she kept agreeing to lighten her tone, but she just couldn't stop harping on courtship as fundamentally sexist. It had become a matter of integrity for her to always make her point. In the end, the producer let her go and hired someone else.

Most people are too timid to put themselves and their beliefs out there as fodder for the masses. It's the writer's job to bear that risk. And it's hard. It requires courage. Some projects demand a level of courage that put them outside the reach of some writers. You are the wrong writer for a piece if you can't "go there" in telling the truth and consequences of certain human choices.

Once a writer brought us a script about conflict between a mother and daughter. The project was unsatisfying: the encounters between the mother and daughter were far too superficial. In our conversations with the writer, it came out that she personally had serious "therapy-indicated" issues with her own mother. She said to us, "I'm afraid where these scenes might take me. What if my mother ever sees this?" Clearly, she wasn't going to be able to be honest in her scenes — maybe ever, but certainly not in time to meet her deadline.

One of the great truths of writing is that every project can be a moment of grace. If, as Plato said, "The unexamined life is not worth living," then the storyteller's life is excruciatingly worthwhile. Stories are better if they have been an occasion of personal growth for the writer. As Flannery O'Connor said about her classic short story "Good Country People," "One of the reasons this story produces a shock for the reader is because it produced a shock for the writer."

Still, some projects are going to require more depth and courage than the writer has in his toolbox. It's grown-up to acknowledge, "I can't write this script yet. Maybe ever."

c. Respecting Your Voice

It should be fairly obvious that some projects are better suited to a particular writing style. In this sense, a writer's style indicates the kind of genres he or she will take to most naturally. Are you funny? Funny enough to write comedy? Are you weird and creepy enough to write horror or suspense? Are you deep enough to write a drama? Are you imaginative enough to produce a fresh fantasy?

Sometimes, a project really requires certain cultural or personal history experience. It's hard to write a movie set in a country or region in which you've never been. You can do it, but the project gets elevated once you visit the place and watch the people engage in the little details that make a script smarter and more alive.

We once worked with a writer who had a script that was set in Spain. But the writer had never been to Spain. The project was okay in terms of plot, but something was missing to push it into the "worth a read" category. Then the writer visited Spain. She came back and rewrote the script such that characters were now munching on *foie gras* and smoky black paella, whereas before they had just been eating "food." She added Basque resentments and buildings half plastered over as scars from the revolution of seventy years earlier. The project grew in arena, characters, and subplots because of her personal experience in the place of her story.

It's not impossible to write a movie set in a Latino family if you are a fourth-generation New England WASP. But it is a greater challenge in what is already a challenging art form.

One of the things writers are always being told is, "Write what you know." On one level, this implies that a writer should be willing to commit to whatever research a project is going to require. The screenwriter should become a funnel into which flows the information from various sources, and out of which flows the pages of the script.

A harder sense of "write what you know" has to do with the psychological or emotional depth of a piece, and whether the writer has the vocabulary for that insight. Knowing what is wrong with someone is a far cry from being able to express what is wrong. It's another level too to be able to dramatize that problem. We tell our writers to "write what [their] soul knows," which means that they have to have articulate insight into the struggles that they are going to set before their characters. This means writers have to journey into the darkness ahead of their characters to be able to visually reflect how the darkness feels and how it acts.

Our rule is to always ask yourself: "Is there a way I can make this project something that *I* can do?" Can you figure out a way to tell the story that is slightly more in your wheelhouse? What life experience can you bring to the table that speaks to the heart of the characters you are writing? Are the producers open to your making their story your own? If your pitch is well prepared, fun, and smart, chances are the answer will be, "You're hired!"

d. Your Passion Project

Many writers start out inspired to write something so deeply personal to them, or so ambitious, that it can take years for them to become the writer they need to be to properly execute their idea. We often see new writers clinging to these projects, struggling to find the story in the idea, frustrated because no one sees their "vision" for the project. What starts out as starry-eyed determination to write something that truly matters to them often fizzles into disillusionment and disappointment. In fact, few writers actually stick it out long enough to really see those projects come to fruition.

Passion projects are special in the sense that there is a deep need for the writer to tell that particular story. Passion projects most often relate back to the elements of a writer's credo, what they truly believe. They speak to the fiber of a writer's being.

We believe that if a writer has a burning desire to write their passion project, then they must absolutely do so. However, if it is the writer's first script, chances are that said project will probably not come together on the first try, or even the second. Many writers, including us, have learned the hard way that starting out with a passion project means years and years of revisions to get it where it needs to be.

If a writer has the self-restraint to start out with a story idea that is much more manageable for their skillset, we highly recommend doing so. We say this knowing that people who have passion projects will probably forge ahead anyway. If you find yourself stuck on a story that you can't let go of, sometimes the best thing you can do is stick it in a drawer, go write a different story, and come back to it when you are a more proficient writer. You are not abandoning your project; you are becoming the writer you need to become in order to do your material justice.

e. The Essential Skills of Storytelling and Screenwriting

These are the "non-negotiables" of proficiency in storytelling for the screen:

1. **A Honed Story Sense** — Writers acquire the "family resemblance" of storytellers in the same way that kids start to act like their parents. The talent is partially embedded in a writer — the way kids inherit genetic material. But starting to look and act and think like a storyteller is equally rooted in hanging around other storytellers. If you intentionally and consistently dwell in the company of people telling tales, chances are good that their sensibilities will start to grow on you.

   In essence, if you want to be a good writer, *read!* Read the stories that have lasted for centuries: the Greek myths and *Aesop's Fables.* Read Homer and the best of the Greek dramas. Read *The Arabian Knights* and *The Canterbury Tales*, the Brothers Grimm and Shakespeare. And Shakespeare. Never stop reading Shakespeare. Read the classics of American and British literature, and study the writings of one or more of the masters such as Dickens, Hawthorne, Austen, Melville, and the Brontës. Read the best of the moderns: Undset, Faulkner, Fitzgerald, O'Connor, Greene, and Hemingway. And Shakespeare. Did we mention Shakespeare?

   Also, *watch!* Know the canon of great cinema. Watch *Metropolis, Casablanca, Citizen Kane*, and *On the Waterfront, Rear Window*, and *The Godfather.* Watch all the Academy Award– and Golden Globe–winning films in the "Best Picture" and "Best Screenplay" categories. Stay current on critically acclaimed films. Watch the best work in the genre for which you are writing.

   If you take on this company as your friends and mentors, it will form your inner story sense. You will begin to feel in your spirit when a plot point just isn't high stakes enough. You will know in a way you might not be able to verbally articulate that a character would never make a certain choice. You will disdain characters who are superficial and lacking in quirky appeal.

2. **Technical Formatting** — A screenplay is a technical document very much like an architectural blueprint. You can't skip learning how to correctly write sluglines any more than an architect can skip how to include electrical outlets in a client's dream house.

3. **Economical, Descriptive Prose** — Good use of language is a skill that all writers require. In screenwriting, language and vocabulary skills are complicated by the need to be strictly concise. Generally, a location should be described in a line or two of key details. A character's visual style needs to be conveyed in about the same. With only 120 pages or fewer in which to tell a whole story, a writer needs to have exactly the right words at hand to set the tone and clearly delineate the action.

4. **Visual Imagery** — In movies, pictures do the bulk of the work of storytelling. The soundtrack can powerfully complement what the audience is seeing, but the main information about character and story has to be told through the character's look and what they do. An essential skill for screen storytelling is finding the right choices for characters to make — things visual and provocative — such that the true stakes and the characters' psychology can be read right through them.

5. **Character Design** — There is a genius to creating quirky, admirable, fascinating characters that are flawed and needy from the same springs from which they are brilliant and powerful. They have to drive their own arc of transformation at the same time that they are fighting an inner battle with the darkness that just might overwhelm them. Beginning writers tend to create characters that are too pathetic or too perfect, too dark or too regular. Mastery in character design means creating someone who is real enough to be relatable, but "better than the real" enough to be entertaining.

6. **Dramatic Structure** — After figuring out what the plot of the story will be, the next biggest decision a writer makes is how to

tell that story. Probably nothing requires as much thought from a screenwriter as structure does. This is because the needs of the audience are pretty much fixed, and there isn't a lot of flexibility in serving those needs. They need to be hooked in the first few minutes. They need rising suspense and major reversals in the first half hour. They need a pulse of steady beats, and then they need a cathartic, purging peak. And, as Aristotle notes in *The Poetics*, it all has to happen before they have to get up and go to the bathroom!

Structure can provide the smartest spectacle in a story, but only because the writer has broken her brain finding the cleverest way to deliver the plot. People learn structure by playing with it. A lot. A writer who doesn't know how to play is not going to master screen storytelling.

7. **A Sense of the Moment** — When we think about movies that we love and that haunt us, the recollection is always tied to key moments in the story. In *Titanic*, it was the scene on the bow. You know the one? Of course you do. In *Raiders of the Lost Ark*, it was Indy shooting the Arabian swordsman. Remember? In *The Godfather* — well, there are many, but who doesn't remember the discovery of the horse head in bed, or the don playing with orange peels with his grandson, or the baptism in which Michael becomes the Godfather?

A great movie is a series of great moments. The story leads in and out of them. They deliver action or character psychology with a richness that separates story from anything real life has to offer. A good writer needs a keen sense of the moments in a story, how to set them up, how long to stay in them, and how to transition the story to the new height that the moment has taken us.

f. Finding Your Voice: An Exercise

A surprising number of writers live in terror of the act of writing itself. The fear is that the well of creativity is going to run dry. Even after twenty-five years of working on top television shows like *M*★*A*★*S*★*H* and *Moonlighting* and *Judging Amy*, and having won a slew of industry awards, writer / producer Karen Hall noted to one of our classes, "Every time I start on a new script, I hear a voice inside saying, 'You'll never be able to do this. This one will show you are a fraud.'"

We have found that half of writer's block has its origin in a writer not having made a project his or her own. Commerciality is at the intersection of a relevant theme and one of the writer's most robust passions. This is the true meaning of "write what you know." The trick for a writer is to make writing more of an experience of recollection, and of description of a story's emotions and psychology, than one consisting of guessing what those same moments might feel like for a piece's characters.

When we hear that a writer is having writer's block, we encourage them to answer a series of questions from an exercise called "The Look Within" by the late writer and screenwriting professor, Delle Chatman, of Northwestern University. It's been very helpful in allowing writers to rediscover their passion and their sense of narrative writing so they may solidify their own story. The questions can help you get a sense of the genres and themes to which you are naturally geared. But most of all, the exercises get you writing in a way that reveals your unique voice and passions as a storyteller.

1. You are standing on the front stoop of a house to which you have been invited as a dinner guest. You knock and are admitted. You meet the family one by one; you eat and observe the family dynamic. Write a first-person account of being a guest in this home. One thing: The house is your house when you were twelve years old.

2. Their beloved child is engaged to be married. There is a dinner to meet the future in-laws. Afterward, they are in the car driving

home and talking about their impressions of their in-laws-to-be
— the little things they noticed — and what they think their
child marrying into that family will mean. Write the conversation. One thing: The future in-laws are your parents.

3. You raise your eyes out of your hands. You look up from the
bench and scan the room. You close your eyes, lean back, and
exhale. "I was always afraid that someday this thing would land
me in jail."

4. They used to hang out — date? — but they don't anymore. Ten
years later, one of them sees the other across the room at a social
event and hesitates before crossing over to reconnect. Write that
person's inner conversation. One thing: The person is the one
who used to be your friend, and it's you who they see across the
room.

5. Whenever the phone wakes me out of a deep sleep, I see your
face. There is a moment of panic until I am sure it isn't someone
calling me to tell me something has happened to you. You are
one person who must not die before me.

6. I'm still not laughing about it. I don't think I ever will.

7. I knew I was in trouble the first time he / she walked in. Why is
it that this is the kind of person I always fall for?

8. They've been married for nine years. One of the partners has
realized that that thing about the other is never going to change,
and it is very boring. It is scary to think of living with it for-
ever. Write the conversation between that person and God. One
thing: That person is your future spouse.

9. If I have to end up a lot like my parents, there is one thing I
don't want to inherit from them.

10. It's been awhile, but when I remember it, it still gives me chills.
I remember the whole thing like it was in slow motion, or like I
was hovering over myself, watching. It still scares me.

11. I will know I am a success as a writer when…

CHAPTER 3

NOTES ON STORY

THE NOTES:

- "Lots of talking and running around in this script, but for what?"
- "The stakes just aren't high enough."
- "It's not edgy enough."
- "What's the hook?"
- "Nothing happens in this story."
- "This doesn't really end. It just stops."
- "Not enough conflict."

The first thing to internalize is that there really isn't anything new here. That is, the elements of story have been in place since the first communities of people. Every ancient society has its stories; and in most of them, stories and storytelling evolved in a very organic, conscious, and even systematic way.

Ancient people organized themselves into self-sustaining communities. The roles of the various members of each tribe were determined by natural gifts and family tradition. Some were designated hunters and soldiers; others were farmers; and others made the shoes and clothes, the wine, the oil, the weapons, et cetera. There were always a few key leadership roles: the chief, the priest, and generally, the storyteller.

Basically, the people of the village would get up every day at the crack of dawn and head into the fields and forests. They would labor in the hot sun or cold frost so that together, they could sustain themselves with the basic needs of human life. But there was one member of the community who didn't go out and sweat beyond the village gates. This was the storyteller. He or she would sit under trees and brood. He would observe the tribe members at their work, and in their relationships with each other. The storyteller would sit around all day and stare and think. Then, at night, after everyone had come in from their work, and had eaten in their tent, the storyteller would wait for his brethren around the fire or near the gates. Now he was on. He had to earn his keep by giving the community one more thing it needed besides food and shoes: a whopping good tale.

The ancients figured out pretty fast that the healthy and productive functioning of their little communities had everything to do with the stories that they shared and enjoyed together. A storyteller was successful if she kept everyone enthralled while providing something important to learn and take away. Stories worked if the hearers found in them something to take to their tent and dream about, providing fuel to head back into the fields and forests the next day. Stories also worked if they allowed the community to jointly process the notions that would make for brotherhood and order in the village. What are the foibles of human nature? What is a virtuous and heroic life? What is true happiness, and where do we find meaning and satisfaction? How should we live together in peace and prosperity?

These basic realities about our need for good tales haven't changed. We still reach for stories in the same way our ancient brothers and sisters did. We still need to engage our imaginations to help us recommit to the mundane parts of human life and responsibility. We still need to discover together what our shared values are. We need to be bonded by the experience of story — thrilled by suspense; amused by the absurdity of the human comedy; saddened by anguish and suffering; terrified by evil; and curious about the mysteries in the cosmos and in our own hearts.

A big part of a writer's job is to serve the needs of the audience in the same way as did storytellers of old. The audience has certain expectations when they buy a story, the way they have expectations when they buy a fish or a cake. Insofar as a writer gives them what their hearts are searching for, he will find success. The storyteller who has the ability to entertain and impart wisdom finds near worship from his society. It's what we today call a fan base. Storytelling requires respect for the common human nature of the audience, and respect for the nature of story itself. A talented writer stretches the storytelling form into new possibilities, but still delivers a story. It's fine for a writer to pursue their own therapy or catharsis in their work, but they shouldn't count on the general public needing to subsidize that enterprise. The good news is: In crafting a solid story to serve the audience's need for wisdom and catharsis, invariably a writer will find his own.

a. A Story Is Better Than the Real

> *I find that most people know what a story is*
> *until they sit down to write one.*
> — FLANNERY O'CONNOR

We have read many screenplays in our years as directors of development, readers for independent production companies, readers for various script and film contests, and mentors for many, many students. Most screenplays that survive the initial test of industry-standard formatting soon fall by the wayside because of problems with the story. **Sadly, the number-one note that really should be given on most screenplays is, "Sorry, but this script should never have been written!"** What fuels such a note is that a particular project has failed in its basic essence. Despite the presence of creative spectacle, intriguing moments, quirky characters, and witty lines of dialogue, the piece never became the thing it was meant to be: a story.

There are many definitions of and formulas for conveying the essential aspects of story. One we like is: "A story is the series of

choices that lead someone from what they want to what they need."
This idea points to the essential notion that story is an internal
and external transformation of character, and probably of location.
Other people speak of story as a lesson, or as a puzzle. But to practi-
cally help writers get to the heart of what the audience enjoys and
expects in a story, we say, "Story is better than the real."

On its most basic level, a story is good in every way in which
it is not real life. Stories need to be at least as good as real life, but
to be successful they must be much better. This is why we reach
for them! We already have real life in all its ambiguity, confusion,
complication, and disorder. We want stories because they offer
something better, a respite from the real that allows us to see aspects
of reality in sharper focus. But in a fun way!

Real life is one long mishmash of lessons and impressions
coming at us without any order or coordination. We are simultaneously learning how it feels to experience jealousy and how that
scourge makes us act out... while we are learning that elderly people
have wonderful perspective... while we are learning how not to
wear dark socks with tan shoes... while we are learning how to
recharge a car battery, et cetera. There is no reason or order to real-
life experience. It comes at us in a jumble, like a tsunami of urgent
lessons, most of which wash over us and don't really change us until
we've been laid low by them many, many times.

When writers hear us say that a story needs to be better than
the real, sometimes they think we mean that we want stories to be
fake. No! If real life has its moments of discomfort, stories need to
be relentlessly gritty. If real life sometimes has a moment of irony
or humor, stories need to be sidesplitting catalogues of the absurd.
Stories need to be at least as good as the real, but a great story tran-
scends real-life experience and imbues it with meaning.

We seek story because it offers us the smorgasbord of life in
digestible servings. Story selects strains of experience and compiles
wisdom about that experience for us in an emotionally engaging
and intelligible way.

Where people in real life are guarded and mysterious to us, story characters are open and accessible. We can know with certainty their hopes and dreams, their foibles, the trail of their failures, and the motivations for every choice they make.

Where people in real life are sheepish, unenlightened, inconsistent, and shiftless, story characters are heroic, quirky, driven, and always entertaining.

Where real life seems to be an endless sequence of the mundane and the repetitious, story appeals because it presents high-stakes, original drama with all the boring parts cut out.

Finally, where real life is disordered, messy, and meaningless, great stories offers beauty: a whole and harmonious unity that delivers wisdom. A great story is always *about* a mess, but can never *be* a mess. A good one is a wondrous thing that lifts the audience high above themselves and their problems so that they can look down and see everything with a new and truer perspective.

b. Story Has a Nature

Twenty-five hundred years ago, the brilliant natural philosopher, Aristotle, plunked down a few pennies for the ancient equivalent of a Coke and some popcorn, and set about the task of watching plays. Really watching. He was sure that plays and stories were important to human culture, so he wanted to know what made a play work technically, and what factors caused an audience to become disinterested and disengaged from a story. He wanted to know how stories impacted audiences and societies for good and evil, and why human beings were drawn to them.

His treatise, *The Poetics,* remains the seminal work on the nature and purpose of story; and although the rhythms and style of classical philosophy are a struggle for the generally crippled and undereducated postmodern brain, we encourage every storyteller to spend a lot of time sitting at the feet of Aristotle with this work. In the end, when a screenplay fails, it tends to be because it ignored some concept Aristotle so blithely dropped in a few words here or there in *The Poetics*. Woe to serious storytellers who disdain this work.

Aristotle lists the essential parts of a story in this hierarchy:

1. Plot
2. Character
3. Theme
4. Dialogue
5. Music / Tone
6. Spectacle

All of the parts are necessary. Story notes often reference the absence of some of these parts. "There is no theme in this piece" or "there is nothing fun for the audience in this project" indicate that a writer has left out one of the defining elements of story. It would be like an architect building a house and forgetting to include the door. It's not going to work.

The order is critical. In a hierarchy, the entities at the bottom are subservient to the elements that are above them. Hence, in a story, all the other parts serve the plot. Certainly, one of the reasons that Hollywood's offerings have become increasingly unsatisfying in the decades since the emergence of the blockbuster is that "spectacle" and "character" (read: "celebrity") have become the most prevalent elements of the story pyramid.

Knowing the individual parts is essential to understanding the larger nature of something. But we need to go further and give a definition that expresses the sum of all of these parts.

A story is the artful telling of an event that happens to a certain individual or group of individuals that is organized around a theme. Each of these phrases is key.

"A story is the artful telling..."

A story is not a slice of life. It is not a camera, pasted to the wall of a bank, watching people listlessly or urgently walk by all day. One of the medium's masters, Alfred Hitchcock, rejected the *cinéma vérité* trend of the 1950s that had filmmakers trying to make movies as close to real life as possible. Hitch noted, "Some people want to make movies that are a slice of life. I prefer to make movies that are a slice of cake."

A cake is put together by a baker choosing certain ingredients for their quality and according to the overall kind of cake that is being made. Elements are brought together like the batter, the filling, the frosting, and the toppings — each in themselves delicious, and together, harmonizing to produce a delicious whole.

Movies and the stories they bear need to reflect the same kind of thoughtful selection of details through a process we call creative control. The teller of the story begins making choices right after typing the words FADE IN. What point of view will I use? What details will I stress? What details can I gloss over? What sequence of telling the details of the story will be most involving for my readers, or in the case of film, my viewers? Is this character twenty or thirty? Do I use the word "shady" or "shadowy"?

"Artful" means skilled. It means that talent is involved. It means that someone has labored over the details of craft; they've practiced and acquired some kind of mastery. It means that a storyteller is an artist.

"Artful" also implies that a story is meant to be a work of art, as in something that is trying to bring a new epiphany of beauty into the world. **Beauty, in the classical sense, doesn't mean "pretty." It means that a project incorporates wholeness, harmony, and radiance.**

1. Wholeness — All the parts are present; nothing is "added on" or extra. Wholeness in a story means that all six of Aristotle's elements are present, and that all of their constituent parts are present as well.

So, in order for a story to work, the plot needs to have several parts, among which are the beginning, the middle, and the end.

Let's just focus on the beginning by considering wholeness. A beginning in a story has several parts, including: the establishment of the arena; the introduction and development of the main character;

the suggestion of the theme; the introduction of the principal inner and exterior conflicts; the introduction of supporting characters (which may include an antagonist); and an inciting incident which launches the action of the plot. All of these are constituent parts of the beginning that are required for the project to be whole so that it might be beautiful.

And it needs to be said that each of those parts of the beginning have several smaller parts. Storytelling is a complex craft, and the beauty of a piece is heightened by complexity.

Wholeness provides a sense of satisfaction to the audience and gives a feeling of rest.

2. Harmony — All of the parts are related in a complementary way. Complementary relationships are those in which the excellence of every part is magnified by how each one brings out the best in the other parts. In a beautiful story, the goal is to have the parts not necessarily be perfect in themselves, but rather be perfect in doing their contribution to the whole project.

The key factor in determining harmony is a project's theme. It is the theme around which all the parts must be harmonized. It is impossible to have harmonization without a controlling idea.

Harmony provides a sense of delight for the audience.

3. Radiance — The intellectual, moral, or spiritual enlightenment that inheres in a project and gives it the gravity that is a mark of the beautiful. The radiance in a work of art is more or less articulate, depending on the wordiness of the art form. A story is probably the most articulate kind of art and, hence, can be the most specific in terms of communicating wisdom and truth.

Radiance satisfies the audience's desire to know.

"... of an event..."

Something has to happen for there to be a story about it. If something is going to happen, then it is happening in time. The event has a moment in which it begins, and a moment in which it ends. A good screen story sweeps the readers in from the beginning, lets them travel through an event, and then leaves them shaking their heads at the end of the event, like they just stepped off of a roller-coaster. In screenwriting, the standard rule is: "Movies *move!*"

At the end of the screenplay, a reader should be able to sum up in a few lines what the event around which you crafted your telling was. A reader will describe a good screenplay by being able to say, "This is a story about the Titanic sinking." You may not know how you are going to craft your telling at the beginning of your writing, but you must know what event you are going to feature as the heart of your tale. You have to know what is going to happen and how it is going to change the arena.

Most beginning screenwriters don't know when to begin their stories. We recommend the rule of good tennis playing: "Hit the ball when it is on the rise." That is, begin your story well into the action. Avoid providing all the backstory and history before your story gets started. Telling a good story on the screen requires briefing the audience about the lives of the characters as though they were going on before, and will continue to go on afterward. We are walking alongside them for a few hours. Let the backstory of the characters unfold with the action, not as a precursor to it.

A good story has resolution and provides satisfaction. It's fine to keep your audience guessing all the way up to the last page. But you have to stop the guessing game on your last page. The audience has to know what happened, and there has to be a sensation of finality to the story. As we say in the business, "Ambiguity — good. Confusing — very bad."

"... that happens to a certain individual or group of individuals..."

All good stories are character driven. Screenplays are about how certain individuals experience an event. People in Hollywood are fond of repeating, "There isn't any new story. It's all in the execution." That is, the three-line story summary matters far less than how that storyline is executed on screen. In most cases, the details of what happens are not the catchy part of your screenplay idea. It's all about the person to whom the event is happening that makes the "what" intriguing.

For example, a good pitch would run, "This is a story about a group of people who shipwreck on a deserted island. Now here's the clincher: The people who get shipwrecked are — you're going to love this — a professor, a movie star, a bumbling captain and his first mate, 'the girl next door,' a millionaire, and his wife." It's not about the shipwreck. It's about the people who are shipwrecked.

Even more than just an event happening to a person, a story is a particular person's slant on a particular event. A story is all about point of view.

An example is the story about the Pied Piper of Hamelin. Take a few moments and imagine the Pied Piper, at the age of 80, looking back on his life and recounting the events that led him to walk into the mountains with a crowd of young children behind him. Seen through the Piper's recollection, who is the villain of the piece? What about the town impels the Piper to abscond with the children, rather than, say, the livestock?

Now tell the story from the point of view of one of the children. Now tell it from the point of view of one of the parents. Now tell it from the point of view of a travelling visitor who picks up the details here and there, years after the event has happened in the town. Every time you switch the point of view, you end up working out a whole new story.

"... that is organized around a theme."

The theme is the unifying idea that gives the whole project its reason to be. The theme is the answer to the question, "What is this movie *really* about?" Confusion in theme makes a project feel incoherent and disjointed. In your first few pages of clever setups and red herrings, you can get away with your reader wondering, "Hmmm, what is this story going to be about?" But if after ten pages a reader is still shaking his head and wondering, "What is this story about?" your screenplay will most likely get a pass.

The theme is the thing that determines the structure. The theme determines which choices are the ones that drive the character's arc of transformation. The theme makes the movie about much more than what *Casablanca* called "the problems of three little people," and instead makes yours a story for every human being.

c. Movie Stories Have a Special Nature

You begin with the possibilities of the material.
— ROBERT RAUSCHENBERG

A movie needs all the elements that go into a story, plus several others that reflect the additional potentials that make up the cinematic art form. **A very common story note is: "This writer wants to be making a documentary." Another is: "This writer wants to write the next *War and Peace*."** Both these notes indicate that the writer doesn't understand the limits and possibilities of screen storytelling.

A movie story needs to include considerations of genre and scope, and needs to be cinematic, dramatic, and economical.

Genre

Genre will be covered more thoroughly in Chapter 8. For our purposes here, know that people tend to make the kinds of movies they like. Audience members tend to buy tickets for the kinds of movies they like. Genre is a commitment to the industry and audience that this story is of a certain type and will pack a certain kind of emotional experience. As a rule, the industry doesn't know how to market "cross-genre" material, and tends to avoid it. It is the writer's job to set the tone of the project early on in the script and then lead the viewers on a dance around a particular emotion.

Scope

Movies tend to be an expensive art form to realize. Hence, a screenwriter needs to have a sense when starting out just how big a piece is going to go. Some stories are epic, and require casts of thousands and monumental set pieces. But no one wants a $200 million script from a beginner. First efforts should be geared to quirky, small human stories that pack a wallop of emotion.

Once a writer is working for a producer, the question of scope becomes very important. If the producer tells you they want a $15 million movie, then it is up to the writer to have a sense of what that means. The story will be shaped partly by these budget considerations in the same way that Michelangelo's *Last Judgment* was dependent on the shape and size of the Sistine Chapel.

Cinematic

There are several ways in which a movie story needs to be cinematic, and these will be covered more thoroughly in Chapter 11. But no matter what, a film story needs to depend on the things that only movies can do to be executed fully. This means that when a writer is adapting a book, serious consideration should be made to what the potentials of the screen offer that will heighten the stuff of the story.

A cinematic story is one that relies on visuals. It utilizes techniques unique to the art form like intercutting, montage, voiceover, non-diegetic sound, camera movement, flashback, and transition. A cinematic story will be layered to take advantage of the fact that a movie can give an audience several different kinds of information at one time.

Dramatic

Cinema draws hugely from theatrical form in terms of structure. Movies don't all need to be written in three acts, but a writer needs to have mastered the three-act structure before straying off this tried-and-true formula. There is something organic in the tri-part formula that works with the rhythms of the human mind. Dramatic structure means that a movie needs to be sensitive to the natural rhythms of the viewer, who needs things like inciting incidents, plateaus, turning points, foreshadowing, setups, and payoffs.

Economical

Cinema is an art form in which the sizes of the canvases are pretty much fixed. Basically, there are short films and there are feature films. Time will tell what might come next, but for the bulk of cinema history, audiences have been served up movies that run around two hours long. Short films seem to be getting shorter all the time, but the norm is somewhere between fifteen and thirty minutes.

A writer needs to conceive a story that can be told in either of these two timeframes. If it doesn't fit — what Aristotle referred to as a "magnitude" problem — the story won't work as a movie.

d. A Story Has to Matter

> Stories are equipment for living.
> — KENNETH BURKE

A story needs to offer the world something to learn, something to feel, and something to dream. Delivering these is the purpose of the storyteller's efforts. They are the core of the "contract with the audience," and also the key to story doing its job in a world driven obsessively to whopping good tales.

Story as Something to Learn

Human beings are innately curious and driven to know. If you don't believe that, lean over in a crowded room and say in a muted voice, "So, last night, I happened to walk by the window, and you'll never guess what I saw! It was unbelievable! There, right smack in the middle of the driveway was —" I promise you that if you stop and look up at that point, there will be several people craning their heads to hear the next part of your story. They want to know what it is you saw. They don't even know yet why they might care, but their interest has been piqued.

As artful depictions of men in action, stories are the privileged way in which human beings learn. That is, the privilege refers to the fact that they are our favorite way to learn. They offer a fun way to grow and collect the wisdom that will make life more navigable, and more comprehensible.

The primary lesson that people want to learn in story has to do with a better way to live. They are setting themselves down at the storyteller's feet, hoping that at the end of the fun and frenzy, they will walk away a deeper, more enriched person. This means that the storyteller needs to think of the fruit of their labors as a parable. It needs to be a vessel channeling wisdom and understanding, or it just won't feel worth it to the audience.

If you are hearing the note, "I don't know what this story means," it's possibly because your characters are failing at point of view. This is a story that refuses to express any values. The audience is puzzling over whether the characters' choices are good and healthy, or destructive. The writer needs to know. Sometimes a failure in point of view happens when a writer is not putting himself into the story's key moments and really plumbing his psychological mindset. Storytellers are not propagandists, but one reason writing requires courage is that the individual must put him or herself "out there" and stand in front of society and say, "This is what I believe."

The arena of a tale offers the audience a fun and free way to absorb knowledge. It's fun and free for the audience, coming along as background flourishes in the story. But satisfying this kind of detailed learning is anything but "fun and free" for the writer. It can require hours of research to pull off an in-depth understanding of the arena that backgrounds your tale.

Think of the film *The Perfect Storm* and how it opened up the unseen world of the North Atlantic fisherman. What does he eat at sea? And where do they store that fish on the boat? And how do they keep it from rotting? And what is the honor code among the scruffy lot of boat hands? And what does it mean to be trapped in a "perfect storm"? It's only through hours of research that a writer can possibly expect to nuance out all the fascinating details that underlie a great story.

So, if you are hearing the note, "This script is a little boring," before you go and add an action sequence, consider deepening the details of your character's profession and environment. It might add the "smart" factor that the whole project is missing. And chances are that as soon as you do, you'll end up finding a smart new direction for the story.

Story as Something to Feel

If the notes coming in about your script are, "Boring!" "Draggy!" "As far from a page-turner as possible!" your project is failing to make an emotional connection. Stories are meant to provide a variety of human experience. Especially emotional experience. Our psyches are programmed for a wide spectrum of emotional sensations, ranging from sidesplitting laughter to gut-wrenching sobs, and from the thrill of wonder to the goose bumps and shrieks of terror. When we feel intense emotions, they can act as a cathartic release or purge.

People's lives are mostly dull. I remember a firefighter telling me that he wanted out of his profession because the "drudge factor [was] too high." I responded to him, "Except for those times you are storming burning buildings, right?" He shrugged and said, "That happens a few times a year, but most of the time we are cleaning our trucks and checking people's gas lines." As a rule, human life settles into patterns of experience that tend to be free of emotional peaks and valleys.

Stories afford us the opportunity to experience the wide range of emotions of which we are capable. By taking on the adventures of a character, we share in their emotional responses; and, if the experience is intense enough, profit from the character's School of Hard Knocks as if it was our own. Tolkien noted that stories allow people to break free of the prison of their workaday world so as to experience the full breadth of their human nature.

A story can fail to engage the audience if it is all movement and plot twists and turns, but lacking any real human moments. Finding the deep and universal emotions in the most pivotal choices the main character makes is crucial. A "moment" is an emotional watershed. If you can't pinpoint them in your story, the audience won't find them either.

If you are hearing the note, "The story never engaged me," consider rethinking the kinds and intensity of conflict in your story. Conflict is the soul of all drama, the center of all emotional experience, and the motivator of all of a character's choices.

Story as Something to Dream

The societal point of story is for audience members to watch the trials and tribulations of a made-up character, and then through their imaginations, import the lessons of that fake man into their real lives. People go into a story to find something useful to take back to their real lives.

Notes that reference problems in this area will be expressed like this: "This script doesn't amount to anything," or, "There is nothing for the audience to do here." Generally, novice writers leave nothing to the imagination of the viewer. There is no mystery, nothing below the surface, nothing for the viewer to chew on while he or she is driving home.

If a story is solid, its deepest meaning is exportable and requires the audience to enter into it and to make it their own. Think about a film like *Schindler's List*. This is a film that was haunting and inspiring for many people, even though none of us today live in the world of Nazi concentration camps. Watching Schindler's selfless courage, the audience had to use their imagination to consider if they would make such a sacrifice in their own, modern lives. Hearing the message, "If only I could have saved one more," the audience wondered — in a vitally important way — which person or people in their real world could be "saved" into a great destiny.

In storytelling, a good ending will feel like a new beginning to the audience. This means that the viewers will return repeatedly in their thoughts to the world of the story. This requires imagination as well as memory. A good story will have people wanting to talk to their friends about it, and buying games based on it, and writing fan fiction about it. And then the industry will make a sequel! And another! And you will soon have a beach house in Malibu!

e. "High Stakes" Mean Death

> *Death is the ghost in the attic of everyone's mind.*
> — FATHER ELLWOOD "BUD" KIESER, film producer

One of the most frequently given notes is, "This story flat-lined; it just didn't have high enough stakes." Ironically, a story that is missing a pulse is probably missing a little bit of death. Because of our inescapable mortality, and the uncertainty we have about what happens after our eyes close for the last time, there is nothing that generates more emotion than death. A good movie is the story of someone warding off some kind of death.

The early Christian saint Irenaeus wrote, "The glory of God is man fully alive." This indicates that there are several different kinds of death possible to a character in a story. It is the task of the writer to make the audience feel that each of these carries stakes as high and irrevocable as physical death.

a) Emotional death — Because of trauma, and then a choice to avoid connection with others, a person loses the ability to feel. A character that has suffered emotional death is incapable of compassion and empathy. He has no awareness of the feelings of others. This person is often cruel.

b) Psychological death — A character that loses their psychological life loses contact with reality. He has no reliable meter of what is true, and substitutes alternate realities to account for his experience. This person is unstable, irrational, and unpredictable.

c) Spiritual death — Generally because of a cultivated relationship with evil, the character that "loses his soul" is someone who has no hope. He has no certainty of anything that is not material, and is grimly aware that the material world is slipping away. This person despairs.

d) Moral death — The character that loses his moral sense can no longer distinguish right from wrong. He has no pole for his choices outside of his own wants and needs. This person is ruthless.

e) Social death — Because he has been so hurt, the character that has experienced social death has lost the ability to relate to others. He doesn't trust, so he can't communicate. This person becomes a recluse.

f) Intellectual death — A character that is perpetually in doubt can eventually lose the ability to process at all. Doubt becomes the only certainty, and all growth becomes impossible. This person lives in paralysis.

g) Physical death — The character's heart stops beating and the brain dies. The soul separates from the body. It's really the least of all the possible deaths.

f. Meeting the Audience's Needs

A note that is not given nearly enough in Hollywood today is, "How will this help the people who see it?" The pastoral and prophetic aspect of the storyteller's vocation has been nearly forgotten in the mad rush for money and spectacle that started with *Jaws* and has defined the blockbuster-movie craze ever since. But it is undeniable that stories have power; and wherever human beings have power, as Spiderman taught us all, "comes great responsibility."

Aristotle lays out in *The Poetics* the main reasons that human beings love and need stories, and why they matter to the healthy functioning of our society. Basically, he says that stories provide the journeys that either lead us into wisdom and solidarity with others, or into darkness and disconnection.

From the standpoint of the screenwriter, Aristotle's key insight is that people are driven to stories by two fundamental instincts: the instinct for imitation, and the instinct for harmony. A writer needs to have both of these in mind when crafting a screenplay.

The Instinct for Imitation

Imitation is the preferred way we humans learn. We learn how and what to do by watching other people doing. Hence, to satisfy this instinct, a story needs to have a character doing things. In the movie *Juno*, we follow the title character through the experience of an unplanned pregnancy so that we don't have to find out what it's like in real life. This is the famous "show, don't tell" requirement that all writing books stress. As Aristotle says, a good story showcases "men in action."

Secondly, for a movie to really be satisfying to an audience, the imitation needs to be profound. The more psychological depth is reflected in the character's choices, the more the piece resonates with the audience. In Juno's case, she recognizes her own immaturity in becoming a mother, but selflessly agrees to go through with the pregnancy because she realizes that her child is a human being "with fingernails." The audience loves it when a movie talks up to them by asking them to really enter into psychologically deep motivations. The audience learns about themselves through this resonance.

A writer needs to have some depth to write deep. Flannery O'Connor called it the writer's ability to stare. The writer needs to be staring fixedly at all of life, taking in how things look and how unseen things manifest. This will allow the writer to magnify and replicate these things on the page.

So if you are getting the note, "This project just wasn't worth my time. It didn't have anything to say," chances are you are failing to satisfy the instinct for imitation.

Stories make us more alive, more human, more courageous, more loving.
—MADELEINE L'ENGLE

The Instinct for Harmony

While a story needs to find its substance through human struggle and experience, it's also true that a story is satisfying to the audience because it gives us order, harmony, excellence, and intelligibility. Aristotle says we seek out beauty the way a duck flies south for the winter.

- Karma — A good story needs to offer the audience intelligibility. In real life, we often don't know why we do the things we do; we don't understand the forces that drive us; we don't get to see the cosmic result of our choices; and we generally take years and years to slowly learn something about ourselves. A good story reverses all of these occurrences, and provides access to character motivations, a connecting thread from mistakes made to lessons learned, and a solid resolution in which all the elements of the character's journey come together in a coherent way. In *The Hunger Games*, Katniss' principal motivation is to save her sister. Even though she is terrified, we understand why she steps forward and volunteers for the Hunger Games.

- Beauty — Stories are also better than real life in that they are ordered for an entertaining tension; they have all the parts they need and nothing boring, irrelevant, or extra; they harmonize all their elements; and they have something definite and meaningful to share. *The Artist* is a recent Academy Award–winning film that is a good story, beautifully told, in which all of the elements come together to bring satisfaction and resolution. The global audience embraced the film mainly as an object of delight. In many ways, the modern era is awash in ugliness, disorder, banality, and stupidity. A good story takes us away from all that, and gives us a more perfect vision of what humans can bring forth.

Therefore, an audience's instinct for harmony will be satisfied when a story communicates something worthwhile in a stylish and enthralling way. The audience comes away from such a work feeling exhilarated, inspired, and grateful — all good things for the smooth continuance of the human family.

If the note is, "This script is a mess," or "This story didn't make sense to me," you are messing with the audience's desire for harmony.

g. The Catharsis of Compassion and the Fear of Evil

Stories work when they lead people into cathartic moments that change them irrevocably for the better.

In the most cathartic type of story, the audience feels empathy with the main character, and walks away from the tale of their woes without harsh judgment for that character. Rather, the audience who has journeyed along with a character walks out of the story and into the world saying, "There but for the grace of God go I."

In Pixar's *Brave*, it is Merida's fight with her mother that causes the young girl to make a grave error in judgment, which thereby causes her mother to be turned into a bear. It is in Merida's journey to make amends for her mistake that we develop empathy for her. Aristotle suggests that we need to have compassionate hearts for the smooth running of the planet, since no matter how wise and disciplined we are, humans will make mistakes. We are not talking about criminal behavior here, but rather the messes we make out of frailty, ignorance, and weakness. When someone in our circle fails in this way, we can't excoriate, isolate, or murder them. If we do, eventually we will all be dead. Instead, we need to be prepped by our stories to understand what drove the other to a regrettable choice, so we can help them recover.

People are more motivated by the fear of punishment than by the attraction of good. A good story will also use the fear of evil to lead an audience to a cathartic moment. Nobody wants to be Denzel Washington's character, Whip Whitaker, in *Flight*, but the audience can make better choices as a result of watching his journey. When we watch a character suffer because of their ignorance or folly, we internalize an aversion for the bad choices that got them there. Hence, watching other people pay for their mistakes partially inoculates us from making those same mistakes.

Creating a moment of catharsis in an audience is the fruit of the skillful execution of a whole list of story elements — basically, everything in this book! But beyond just mastery of craft, catharsis results from the following attributes in a story:

- Engagement of the audience with a character who is good, appropriate, consistent, and true to life.
- The character moves initially from good fortune to bad fortune through weakness, ignorance, or folly, as opposed to evil.
- The most important moments of insight in the story come as a surprise.

h. Things Story is NOT

- **Story is not random musings** about an event or emotion or psychological experience. That kind of project may be an interesting work of art, but random musings have almost nothing to do with the structured, intentional nature of story. To say it another way, "Story is not 'a show about nothing.'"
- **Story is not a "day in the life" recording.** Story adds point of view and edits out inessential details.
- **Story is not a series of conversations.** In story, dialogue exists mainly to reveal character. What characters say means nothing beyond what they do.
- **Story is not a literal recounting of an event.** Aristotle distinguishes between history and story by noting that history is something that happened once to a person or group of

persons, whereas story is something that could happen to any person at any time.

- **Story is not a writer's personal therapy session.** A writer can certainly brood over personal issues in a story, but navel-gazing is rarely fun for the person who has to witness it. And story needs to be entertaining to others.
- **Story is not a cool place or fascinating situation.** An intriguing arena is the necessary setting for a story, but just setting up a world is not enough.
- **Story is not a straight line.** A tale without reversals is what is called a "simple plot." A better tale, called a "complex plot," is one with lots of reversals. But even in simple plots, there still needs to be rising action and emotion that peaks and then resolves.
- **Story is not something that just stops; it ends.** A story is over when the idea of the theme has played out and the main character has been irrevocably changed. A theme-less story doesn't know when it is over, so it just kind of meanders around and then stops with a telltale jolt.
- **Story is not just a product to sell.** It is a journey to be shared.

i. Exercises for Crafting Your Story

1. Briefly write the central plot event around which your story will be crafted. (So, for example, you decide to write a story about a family that goes on a vacation to Mexico. They have become alienated and distant from each other, and the father of the family is hoping the shared fun will bring them back together.)

   a) List five kinds of death that you could add to give the story higher stakes. See how many you can add into your story. (If your story is about a family taking a trip to Mexico, you could add that just as they are leaving, the mother of the family asks her husband for a divorce.)

b) Next, come up with five unpredictable reversals that will complicate the beginning of your story of that event. Pick the one that feels the most fresh, like something you have never seen before. (Just as they arrive in Mexico, they accidentally insult the wife of a powerful drug lord.)

c) Next, come up with five complications that could take place in the middle of the story. See if you can work all five into your plot. (The youngest child gets lost in a Talavera tile factory.)

d) Finally, describe five possible ways for the story to end. Throw them out and come up with five more. Use the most surprising and profound on the list. (The father stays behind in Mexico with the wife of the drug lord.)

2. List two or three successful movies that will feel to the audience the way you want your story to feel. What in your story will create the same tone and emotional quality as these other films? (It's *National Lampoon's Vacation* meets *Rocky*...)

3. Complete these sentences:

My story will entertain the audience by _____.
It will satisfy their desire for depth by _____.

CHAPTER **4**

ARENA NOTES:
A WORLD TO EXPLORE

THE NOTES:

- **"Boring."**
- **"Can we set it somewhere else? Anywhere else?"**
- **"I feel like we've seen this movie a thousand times."**
- **"Seems like the writer didn't do her research here."**

Location informs behavior. Imagine your toddler having a temper tantrum in a fancy restaurant. How might you respond to your child? How might your response change if you were at home? In front of your mother-in-law? In front of your boss?

The setting of a story informs how your characters will act, and whether or not they are behaving according to the rules of the place. Setting also informs the audience what your story's "stakes" are. If you are doing your nails at home, the potential for conflict is low. If you are doing your nails in the middle of your boss' business presentation, the potential for conflict is higher.

An arena can be a physical, philosophical, or moral setting for your story. A good arena will influence how your characters react and respond to each other.

The best arenas are specific. Hollywood line producers are often tasked with finding a "standard location" in which to shoot a scene. Part of this comes from the fact that television is so focused on legal and medical procedurals that nearly every show needs to end up either in a hospital lobby or a courtroom. But there is also the ever-present need in the entertainment business for living rooms, classrooms, restaurants, bars, and bedrooms. The industry has too often fallen prey to pressing financial and efficiency requirements, sacrificing the complementary power of a unique arena in favor of just finding actors a basic background in front of which to do their thing.

Think more on how the world of your story can add to the viewer's experience. If your story is set in a café, consider whether the café is an ivy-draped bistro on a cobblestone street, or the gutted-out greasy spoon by the docks after a hurricane. There should be no "standard location" in your story in the same way that there should be no "standard character." Even if the plot unfolds in a "classroom" or a "bar" or a "courtroom," it is the writer's task to come up with a few details that make this classroom, bar, or courtroom completely distinct, and even fascinating. Keep in mind, however, that there is a high demand for economy of language within a screenplay. Unlike novels, where whole pages can be devoted to setting a scene, most screenplays require it to be done in one sentence or less.

Think of the courtroom in *To Kill a Mockingbird*. It is as dusty and creaky and unrefined as the spirit of the bigoted citizens who are gathered there for the trial. Now, recall the crisp and efficient courtrooms that background the *Law & Order* series. These courts are professional places where serious people wrestle with serious crime.

When crafting an arena, a gifted storyteller makes it a place that drips with lots of symbolic alleys and intriguing doorways. Potential complications lurk throughout the story world and are there for the writer when the second act starts to feel flat.

Develop the habit of complicating your arena by making it specific in some way early on. There should never be a "standard location" in your screenplay.

- It's not just a house in ancient Rome. It's a teeming estate completely consumed by a thriving olive oil business.
- It's not just an apartment in Manhattan. It's a former insane asylum one flight up from a Vietnamese restaurant on the edge of Little Italy.
- It's not just an army base. It's in Taiwan during the typhoon season.
- It's never just "Main Street, U.S.A." It's a failed steel town with rust everywhere, or a border town with illegals running across yards, or a seaside vacation spot with a water-table problem.
- It's not just a school. It's a maritime science academy that has classes on a ship.

> *Fairy-stories deal largely with simple or fundamental*
> *things, untouched by Fantasy, but these simplicities are*
> *made all the more luminous by their setting.*
> — J. R. R. TOLKIEN

The arena should complement the tone and scope of a story. Epic movies require epic settings. Where would *Lawrence of Arabia* be without those shots of vast sand dunes? If you are going to take me to sprawling landscapes, you better have a sprawling story and a serious theme. Small, quirky indie films do best when they have something metaphorical in their settings. It was genius in *Being John Malkovich* to set the story in the cramped half-floor of the business office that paralleled the main character's brain.

Arena is a big part of the "Something to Learn" spectacle in a story. We have noted that humans are a kind of being that desire to learn, and that stories are the privileged means by which they do so. Well, arena is one of the key ways in which we can satisfy that need. It requires a writer to do their homework about the world of the story, and then put things into the background that will allow viewers to learn (perhaps without realizing they are being taught). This is the opera music prominent in *Moonstruck*, *Amadeus*, and *Pretty Woman*. It is the commentary on the Revolutionary War in *The Patriot*. It is the inner workings of a Cold War–era nuclear submarine in *The Hunt for Red October*. It is the weird world of prosthetic devices in *The Fugitive*. Determine to teach your audience something factual in your movie, and do it through the arena.

Good arenas have boundaries. Consider the modern-day arena structure of a football stadium. When you watch a football game, you expect the action to take place within the limitations of the field. If the game were occurring in the locker room or the parking lot, it would be out of place, and certainly not worth the price of admission. Great physical boundaries are evidenced in *127 Hours*, which primarily takes place where the main character is literally stuck between a rock and a hard place, or in Hitchcock's *Rear Window*, where the limitation of information that can be observed from Gregory Peck's window informs the entire story.

An arena is a philosophical or moral setting of a story. *To Kill a Mockingbird* works because it takes place in the Depression-era South, where the attitudes of the day create the conflict of the story. If it were set it modern-day Manhattan, there wouldn't be much of a story. In the same vein, the modern-day Manhattan setting of *Sex and the City* works because it speaks to the attitudes of its place. It would be completely ridiculous if set in the Depression-era South. Consider how your character's beliefs and behaviors inform your setting, and whether your setting creates enough dramatic tension for your story.

Arena informs the theme of a story. The theme in *Citizen Kane* is, "What does it profit a man to gain the world and lose his soul in the process?" A theme like this requires Kane to suffer in the monstrous pile of riches that he's acquired. Without the building of his palace, Xanadu, there would be no theme. Consider how the story would be different if Kane were camping out in a modest two-bedroom bungalow at the end. Maybe he'd still be happy. Maybe he'd still have Rosebud.

Arena cannot be extracted from a story. If you can take the story on which you are working and set it anywhere else, it means that the arena isn't quite working for you yet. Think about what your arena *means*, and find ways to make it mean something more.

a. Arena Exercises

1. Watch several movies in the genre that match the story you want to write. What are the settings? What makes the settings unique? Could these stories be told elsewhere? How do the arenas contribute to the plots and choices of the characters?

2. Describe in a few words the world of your story. (i.e., a bar in Chicago)

    a) Move your arena to more specific neighborhood. (i.e., a bar in Chicago's South Side)

    b) Change the economic level of your arena. (i.e., a rundown bar in Chicago's South Side)

    c) Add some history to your arena. (i.e., a rundown bar in Chicago's South Side that used to be a hangout of Al Capone)

3. Try and add some complicating factor into the environment of your arena. It's monsoon season, or unseasonably hot and humid, or the characters are trapped in a frigid ice storm. There is a huge county fair going on across the street, or a political rally, or the demolition of a landmark building.

4. Find something in the arena of your story to metaphorically represent your theme or the main character's struggle. (i.e., Your main character is a postal worker who carries the burden of his brother's death. His mailbag is so heavy, he walks doubled over. He drinks at a bar named "The Albatross." He's desperate to move out of the "City of Brotherly Love," but can't.)

5. Find another movie that is set in the same general locale as your story. How is your arena different and fresh from that earlier film? (i.e., Your story is set in Paris. How is your story uniquely different from *Ratatouille*, or *Midnight in Paris*, or *The Hunchback of Notre Dame*?)

CHAPTER 5

NOTES ON CHARACTER:
THE LOVABLE PARADOX

THE NOTES:

- **"I didn't care about the characters."**
- **"I didn't know what the characters wanted."**
- **"The characters never seemed to change."**
- **"I didn't believe the characters' choices."**
- **"The characters seemed wooden."**
- **"The characters weren't active."**

The essential concern when creating characters is "relatability." It's a Hollywood word for "I get this person and I care about him or her." If the audience does not connect with the characters, then they will spend the whole story witnessing the action — not experiencing it. There is some emotion to be had in witnessing events, but it doesn't make anywhere near the entertaining or formative impact that participation does.

The goal is to create characters that experience catharsis or an emotional release; and who, in turn, create catharsis for the audience. The cathartic effect of storytelling depends on how well the main character represents the audience. The viewer needs to feel so united with the main character that the journey unfolding on the screen may as well be unfolding in his or her own life. If successful, this means that the audience will travel the emotional journey of the story along with the characters and come away steeped in the same wisdom that the character has imbibed. For this reason, anti-hero stories very rarely achieve catharsis in the audience. For every one *Unforgiven* that succeeds, there are a hundred like *Death Wish* that fail. An antihero is distancing to the audience member who thinks that they are basically a good person. Humanizing an anti-hero is basically what antihero movies are about. A cathartic movie needs a flesh-and-blood human being from the get-go.

It needs to be said that not every movie is meant to be a cathar-tic experience. But the best movies — the ones that win awards, critical acclaim, and the loyalty of the mass audience — tend to be the ones that offer an experience of renewal, redemption, and depth.

Achieving the level of connection that will foment catharsis between the audience and the main character is the sum of sev-eral elements. All of them are necessary to ensure that the cathartic impact is not lessened.

a. Qualities of a Relatable Character (Adapted from Aristotle's *Poetics*)

1. **Goodness** — Most people, in spite of how they behave, think they are basically good. The illusion of fiction depends on this. The audience makes choices out of a basic desire for good for themselves and their circle of influence. They can't put their trust in a main character without a similar certainty of basic orientation toward the good. The saying in Hollywood is, "The audience will care about a character who cares about something besides themselves." Implicit in this idea is that the character is not a narcissist and somehow has the welfare of others at heart.

It's important to note that the character can be wrong in his understanding of morality, but that he needs to sincerely pursue good even in his ignorance. An example of this type of charac-ter is Sulley from *Monsters, Inc.* In the beginning of the movie, Sulley shares the prejudice of all the other monsters regarding the dangerousness of humans. He also is too trusting of his bosses in the scare factory, and so is being manipulated by them. We see all of this as we meet Sulley, but we also intuit that he is still basically a good guy. He really cares about his friends and would be loath to do harm to anyone. His scaring of little humans is coming out of his ignorance, and not out of malice.

It's a *huge* point. **Relatability requires that a main character's flaws be found in his folly, ignorance, or weakness, and not in a real attraction to evil.** As Aristotle says, "The most effective plots are those in which a good man suffers bad fortune through weakness or folly."

The folly of a character generally springs from his or her struggle with darkness, which is most easily thought of in terms of the Seven Deadly Sins. It should never be that the hero is innately good and the villain is innately bad. But they are distinguished by the internal battles they are each fighting. That marks the hero. It is the very struggle with his or her darkness that makes a character most relatable to the audience. A villain is one who embraces his darkness. A hero is one who hates his darkness. A villain's real menace comes from the fact that he is not sidetracked or distracted by an inner struggle, as is the hero.

A character that is wed to evil may be fascinating to watch, as in the case of Hannibal Lecter; but if we are going to learn from *Silence of the Lambs*, we need the self-examining, basically moral, and eventually heroic Clarice through whom to journey.

2. **Propriety** — As our society strays more and more from any sense of tradition and moral norms, it becomes harder to explain this very key aspect of relatability. In essence, saying that a character needs propriety means that the audience must find the character trustworthy and basically sane. Propriety means that a character's point of view makes sense to the audience such that the audience puts faith in it. And takes it on. An appropriate character is quirky, but not offputtingly weird.

This all comes from the innate fear people have of looking like fools. No one wants to be the poor guy standing in the middle of the restaurant with a long train of toilet paper stuck on his shoe. An appropriate character makes the audience feel that they are safe and in good hands. They may be challenged, but they are not going to be duped or seem ridiculous.

In order to establish propriety, the audience needs to see the character correctly assess the reality of the world around him or herself in an early scene. We need a bit of resolute grit and truth. This is Nemo's daddy, Marlin, in *Finding Nemo*, fearfully but correctly warning his son about all the dangers lurking beyond the reef. This is Forrest Gump saying over and over, "I'm not a smart man." This is Chaplin's Little Tramp, understanding immediately in *The Kid* that the abandoned child has innate value and dignity. This is Maria in *The Sound of Music* rallying her nerve and prospects in the song, "I Have Confidence."

3. **Consistency** — A huge part of being trustworthy is living up to expectations. In a story, the audience needs to have access to the main character's motivations so as to be able to follow why he does the things he does. Nothing messes with an audience's slipping into a narrative like an unmotivated choice. Characters need to be consistent and comprehensible in the "better than the real" way that most real people are not.

Part of consistency in creating a character is ensuring that they are almost obsessive about achieving their particular goal in the story. A story world offers the luxury of every scene and choice being geared to the character's principal desire or need. Aristotle calls this "unity of plot," and it is an essential ingredient of preserving cohesion within the story. A consistent character will be working on one main internal problem during the story, even if their external problems are many and varied.

Another aspect of consistency is that the character has a known genius. In *Dead Man Walking*, the wonderful character of Sister Helen has a quality (derived from both nature and her state in life) of always saying "yes" when people ask something of her. Her initial "yes" to become a nun led to many more yeses in her life of service to the poor; this momentum is why she responds "yes" when death-row convict Matthew Poncelet calls for her help.

Furthermore, even when a character's flaw is inconsistency, Aristotle notes that that character needs to be consistently inconsistent in order for the audience to understand them.

4. **Truth** — Another key element that determines trust is commonality of experience. If you have been diagnosed with cancer, it means everything if someone comes to you and says, "I know what you are going through. I am a cancer survivor." Suddenly, that person carries a voice of authority that other non-cancer patients simply cannot have.

A relatable character will be one who, at their core, is struggling with a universal human dilemma with which the audience can assent. The character's folly needs to be a particular application of the general struggles with which all human beings are tempted, regardless of culture, era, or demographic. This is Luke in *Star Wars* needing to idolize his absent father, even though his story is set "a long time ago in a galaxy far, far away." This is Salieri's madness-inducing struggle with jealousy in the royal court of seventeenth-century Vienna in *Amadeus*. This is Rick's need to overcome the bitterness that has shut him down in WWII–era *Casablanca*. The audience will trust a character insofar as that character is struggling with something that the audience knows is real and serious.

A true character will point the audience toward whom they could be, and who the society needs them to be if we are to achieve our common destiny.

b. Character Versus Characterization

A character has two levels of qualities: those on the level of character, and those on the level of characterization. The entertainment value of the character — really the heart of our fascination with them — is found in characterization. Relatability is found in character. This is ironic because it is details of characterization that provide the easiest level of connection between people. But this kind of superficial connection doesn't lead to trust. In the end, it is matters of an individual's character that are the most defining, and hence make for more profound connections between people.

Characterization includes all the necessary details about the backstory and the reality of the character. A good story lets us know where the character grew up and how smart she is. We need to know that she drives a '78 Camaro, and that she has a PhD in chemistry. It can add to the fun of the movie that she roots for the Red Sox and that she does a lot of bird-watching in her free time.

In good stories, characterization is complicated with paradox. So the bun-wearing, trim librarian leaves work and takes off full throttle on her shiny red Ducati motorcycle. The huge, blue, long-toothed monster is deathly afraid of toddlers. The concert pianist is going deaf. The bespectacled, legalese-speaking judge collects crazy cuckoo clocks.

All of these facts set up the world around the character and lay out a lot of tools with which they will be handling their oncoming crisis. And while a lot of these can make the audience feel more intrigued by the character, relatability is not necessarily to be had in any of them.

Ultimately, relatability has to do with trust. And while a degree in engineering may make a person trustworthy to design an elevator, it's irrelevant if someone is trying to decide if they should let that engineer babysit their kids. Deciding who to trust as a babysitter has everything to do with knowing a person's character. It's the same with an audience allowing themselves to identify with a main character.

Early on in a story, the positive defining values of the character must be revealed so that the audience can trust him or her. Defining values include the answers to questions like, "For what would this person die?" and "To what would they dedicate their life?" and "How do they act when they are alone?" and "How does this person act in a crisis?" The writer needs to have thought through all of these things.

It isn't necessary for the audience to share the defining values of a character to take that character to heart. But the audience needs to understand that the character *has* defining values, and that he or she is ultimately oriented toward the "good" side.

c. What Do They Want? What Do They Need?

One of the most common notes we give writers is that we aren't sure what a character wants. It is a key note, because the heart of a story is taking a character from what they want to what they really need. The audience needs to get a real sense of the character's folly in wanting the wrong thing in order to have a sense of where that character really should be headed.

A character's want is what drives him into the central action of the story. The best wants are tangible or specific: a Red Ryder BB gun (*A Christmas Story*); to win the pageant (*Little Miss Sunshine*); to exact revenge on the six-fingered man (*The Princess Bride*). The want is often something selfish but endearing; and it is what fuels the action of the movie. The character's goals, fed by the want, are what drive the story forward. Actors will translate this into their "motivation," so it is important to give your actors something to do! The story starts when a character's want is identified, and the story moves forward when the character makes a plan to get what he wants.

When a character wants something that is not tangible or specific, it can be very problematic in screen storytelling. Passive or unspecific wants like "my character wants to be understood" or "my character wants world peace" are problematic. These are very difficult things to dramatize in a visual way for the screen. Likewise, the pursuit of what the character wants must be specific and clear.

Equally problematic is a story in which the writer never really makes clear why the character isn't achieving their goal. It has to be expressed very clearly: What are the real internal and external obstacles standing between the character and what he or she wants? The stakes of the story are all about the shape and depth of those obstacles.

There's a reason why formulaic kid shows, like *Dora the Explorer*, become wildly popular. What does Dora want? To get the baby gorilla back to her mommy. What's Dora's plan? To go over the rainbow bridge, through the dark forest, and into the green, green jungle to Mama Gorilla's house. While your story might (hopefully) be more complex, there should be a clear plan of action your character concocts. As fantastic and longwinded as the *Lord of the Rings* trilogy is, it all boils down to a hobbit who has a clear goal: to take the ring and throw it into the fires of Mount Doom.

As we noted above, most of the time, a character's want, while it might be noble, is not necessarily what's best for him. In the course of a story, a character will set out to get one thing, but invariably learn that he *needs* something different. A character's need is often something internal, but specific. The need is what drives the inner transformation of the character. The character is often not aware (at least, not at first) of his or her need, but the audience usually has some insight into what it is early in the first act.

When a hero goes on a transformational journey, he often learns along the way that what he wants is not the same as what he needs. In fact, he often must sacrifice what he needs in order to get what he wants.

In tragedies and antihero stories, a character transforms from basically good to basically evil by sacrificing what he needs in order to get what he wants. An evil character will go after what he wants — at any cost.

In *A Christmas Story*, Ralphie wants a Red Ryder BB gun for Christmas. He thinks Christmas will be ruined if he doesn't get one. When he does actually get the gun, the first thing that happens is exactly what everybody predicted all along: he shoots his eye out! In the course of the story, he learns that getting what he wants is not really what he needs. His need is to celebrate Christmas with his family, which he does, in a Chinese restaurant after the dog eats the turkey.

Some questions to consider:

- What does my character want?
- Why does he want it?
- Why can't he have it?
- What does he consistently do because of his struggle to get what he wants?
- What internally is standing in the way of him getting what he wants?
- What externally is standing in the way?
- Does he succeed or fail?
- What does this character need?
- What does he do because his need is driving him?
- At what point does my character become aware of his need (if ever)?
- What internally is standing in the way of him obtaining what he needs?
- Will he sacrifice what he wants to get what he needs, or vice-versa?

d. Backstory: How Did They Get Here?

Some of the most informative prewriting you can do consists of developing a backstory for your characters. We often find that writers will struggle with their dialogue and conflict between characters if they don't have enough backstory developed for them. Backstory is very closely linked to creating better subtext, and in finding the voice of your characters. If you are struggling with dialogue, make some backstory decisions to find your character's voice.

At the very least, for each of your main characters, you should know:

- Where and when were they born, and what was the world like outside their door?
- Who raised them, and what was it like at their dinner table every night?
- How much money and material wealth did they grow up with?
- How smart are they, and how much education do they have?
- What have they spent most of their free time doing?
- What major life events have shaped them into who they are today?

Our friend, playwright Buzz McLaughlin, offers some great exercises for creating backstories in his book *The Playwright's Process*. The best is called **The Milestone Exercise.** Starting with your character's date of birth, identify at least six to eight major milestone events that led up to his or her present-day life. What are the key moments that shaped this character? For each of these moments, Buzz recommends writing a monologue from your character's point of view that describes the event. Focusing on key, formative moments will offer great insight as to how your character thinks and views the world around him.

When working on backstory between two or more characters, you need to know where and how they previously met, and what circumstances or conflicts they've already encountered. If you do the Milestone Exercise, you'll likely find that two main characters will share a past event. If two characters have not met until the occurrence of your story, then find how their backstories can still create tension, i.e., one character has a giant St. Bernard because a big dog made her feel safe as a child, and the other has an extreme fear of dogs because one bit her when she was four.

Knowing backstory also informs where your story should begin. A story goes into motion at the inciting incident, which is the major event that shakes up ordinary life for the main character. A story should begin at the moment just before the inciting incident, which will best set up how that moment will change his or her world. We often find writers start their stories way too early because they are still trying to work out backstory. There's often way too much unnecessary information frontloaded onto their story that bogs it down. Backstory is revealed throughout the present story as the audience learns more about the characters.

Another ironic problem in screenplays is too much research and backstory work getting in the way of telling a simple story focused upon a theme. The pitfall of biographical and / or "true life" stories is that they become "episodic" because there is just too much cool backstory that the writer is trying to serve, but which, in the end, doesn't relate to the focus of the main story. The Spielberg movie *Lincoln* fell victim to this repeatedly. The movie never really decided whose movie it was — Lincoln's or Thaddeus Stevens' — and so there were a lot of (ultimately irrelevant) really cool visuals and neat moments that made the whole piece a bit of a slog. The audience didn't know how to put these fragments together.

In deference to what Aristotle called "unity of plot," writers need to make brutal decisions to serve the plot they have chosen. There simply isn't enough time to address everything there is to know about someone in a two-hour movie. Writers in this genre need to know the major milestone events that formed a character — but they also must be resigned to leave lots and lots of cool stuff on the mental cutting-room floor.

If you find yourself struggling to tell your story, constantly refer-ring to other backstory events to explain the present day, there are two things you can do. One is to write scenes that take place in the backstory in order to find a direction for your present story. Another is to change your story to become the backstory event. The best stories are the moments in a person's life that are the most transformative and spectacular. If something more interesting happened in your character's past (or future) than the story you are currently writing, then it's best to change your story to revolve around that moment.

e. Finding the Haunting Paradox

After having established sympathy between your main character and the audience, there is still no greater element to provide plain old fun and entertainment than paradox in the main character. We love stories for many reasons, but one of them is because we love to make new friends out of the fascinating people they bring into our lives as characters. The key to engaging the audience through character is to make your character a living, breathing paradox.

The word "paradox" comes from the Greek for "to think more." The writer and theologian G. K. Chesterton was a master at creating intriguing and hilarious paradoxes as a way of drawing his readers' minds into the contemplation of important truths. He noted, "Paradox is the truth, standing on its head, begging for attention."

That is, you might walk by a person standing on the street and never even give him a second look. But if that person stood on their head without warning, suddenly your attention would be riveted to them. They've suddenly gone from uninteresting to entertaining.

In the same way, putting a paradox at the heart of a character gives that character a fascinating inner contradiction that will set him at war with himself, and provide a mountain of fodder over which the audience can enjoyably brood.

The best paradoxes are those that make a character's strongest quality the source of his most troubling flaw. The trait can't be wished away without the character losing his or her greatest strength. It's fun stuff to set an audience spinning, first asking that they admire a quality, and then that they bemoan it.

Some of the greatest screen characters are examples of this dichotomy. Scarlett O'Hara in *Gone With the Wind* has a will of iron that allows her to survive the ravages of the Civil War. Paradoxically, her strong will also refuses to allow her to quit her absurd and ill-fated obsession with Ashley Wilkes.

In *As Good As It Gets*, Melvin Udall's qualities of perception allow him to identify and address the needs of Carol, his love interest. Paradoxically, it is the same depth of insight that allows him to craft the biting observations that drive Carol (and everyone else) away from him.

In *Babette's Feast*, it is the sister's religious faith that compels the characters to open their home to the refugee Babette. Paradoxically, it is that same religious fervor which nearly drives them to reject the tremendous gifts that Babette has to share.

In *Finding Nemo*, it is Marlin's solicitude for his son that ensures that he will pursue him to the ends of the ocean. Paradoxically, it is Marlin's solicitude which, fueled by too much urgency, drives little Nemo to swim far past the reef and into the net of an unseen boat.

Because of their inner paradox, each of these characters is fighting themselves. This is by far the most fascinating and terrible kind of struggle to behold, thereby yielding the stuff of highly entertaining stories.

f. Character Exercises

1. Write out five peripheral aspects of your character — parts of his characterization. If you have seen any of these in preexisting characters, tweak them until they are all fresh. (i.e., The cute blond girl who puts artichoke tapenade on everything and has a slight lisp.)

2. Write a sentence or two about the character's defining genius. Come up with a conflicting, paradoxical struggle that comes from that same quality. (i.e., Ratatouille is a master chef... who is a rat.)

3. Make a list of at least five active choices your character makes to indicate his character. (i.e., He kicks his sister's dog.) Next, think of five more active choices. Integrate as many of these as possible into your story.

4. Make a list of the five worst things that could happen to your character. Articulate why these particular things would really strain the character you have created. Then work at least three of them into your story.

5. Choose a theme song for your character. Is it "My Way" or "Life in the Fast Lane" or "Don't Worry, Be Happy" or something else?

CHAPTER 6

NOTES ON DIALOGUE:
BETTER THAN REAL SPEECH

THE NOTES:

- "Real people don't talk like this."
- "Really clunky dialogue."
- "It doesn't sound 'fresh.'"
- "The characters all sound the same."
- "Too many 'talking heads.'"
- "Too much awkward exposition."
- "Everybody here says exactly what they are thinking all the time."

Dialogue is a necessary evil.
— FRED ZINNEMANN

The number-one rule of storytelling for film is that it must be visual. In the early days of silent film, some of the best stories were told precisely because they were uninhibited by dialogue. Dialogue is a key component to story, but it is often given too high a place in screen storytelling. In fact, dialogue can often hamper a story. Before dialogue, one must have compelling characters and a foolproof plot upon which to hang. Good dialogue is complementary to the characters and plot.

In the same way that story is better than real life, dramatic dialogue is great in every way in which it isn't real speech. Dialogue offers us language as art, and art takes time and practice, talent and brooding. If real speech is plain, direct, unclear, and inarticulate, dialogue is concise, pithy, authoritative, rhythmic, metaphorical, eloquent, and witty.

A character's style of speech should be directly tied to his or her wants and needs. So if a character is someone who wants approval, her speech will be more timid, always agreeable, and less confrontational and dogmatic. If, on the other hand, a character wants to be his own man, his speech will be brusque, challenging, and assertive. In short, you can't write dialogue for a character until you know who they are.

Here are some specific ways that dialogue is better than real speech:

a. Dialogue Is Designed to Be Heard

Dialogue in a story should be an earful. It should be memorable for the very way it sounds. Different characters should have different cadences to their speech. If they were instruments, some characters could be thought of as violins — whiny and high-pitched — and some as throbbing basses. Different emotional effects can be elicited from the contrasting sounds of characters' voices.

Think of the thick, slow, almost rasping tones of Marlon Brando's Godfather. They provided a marked contrast to the sounds produced by the other characters around him, and they gave his character more presence in the movie.

If you are getting the note that "All the characters sound the same," an easy fix is to give one of your characters a lisp or an accent or a halting pattern of speech — anything to break up the monotone.

Human beings like repetition. Because we have the ability to detect patterns, we tend to enjoy them when we hear them. How else to explain the success of the Beach Boys? They made millions serving up silly word patterns set to catchy tunes. "Ba-ba-ba-ba-ba-bar-b'ra Ann," or "Help me Rhonda, help, help me Rhonda."

Word repetition or phrase patterns in dialogue will take different forms, depending on the genre. If the words call attention to themselves, they are probably being overdone. Yet this sort of wordplay can create a great deal of fun in a movie.

(From *Patton*[1])

> PATTON
> Nobody wins a war by dying for his country. You win a war by making the other poor bastard die for <u>his</u> country.

(From *Double Indemnity*[2])

> PHYLLIS
> I wonder if I know what you mean.

> WALTER
> I wonder if you wonder.

(From *A Few Good Men*[3])

> DANIEL
> I want the truth!

> COLONEL JESSUP
> You can't handle the truth!

(From *The Fugitive*[4])

> RICHARD
> <u>I</u> didn't kill my wife.

> SAMUEL
> <u>I</u> don't care.

---

[1] 20th Century Fox, 1970, screenplay by Francis Ford Coppola and Edmund H. North
[2] Paramount Pictures, 1944, screenplay by Billy Wilder and Raymond Chandler
[3] Castle Rock Entertainment, Columbia Pictures, 1992, screenplay by Aaron Sorkin
[4] Warner Bros., 1993, screenplay by Jeb Stuart and David Twohy

(From *Glengarry Glen Ross*[5])

> AARONOW
> Are you actually talking about this,
> or are we just — ?

> MOSS
> No, we're just...

> AARONOW
> We're just "talking" about it.

Clearly, real people do not talk like this. In real life, we would have no patience for this kind of back and forth. It's the kind of wonderful dialogue that is so much better than the real that it makes the audience forget that anybody who actually talked like this would probably be encouraged to seek therapy.

b. Dialogue Is Designed for Actors to Play

Play. There's that word again. Dramatic stories should be fun. Unlike real speech, a dialogue scene needs to have enough scope that the actors can find something entertaining therein. It needs to suggest physical gestures and expressions. It needs to have a style that suggests the character's inner psyche in such a way that there is room for the actor to exaggerate, understate, and get really emotional. Actors want rich lines that they can plumb and find three or four different ways of delivering. **The writer's words have to provide a sturdy enough frame to support the actor's emotions.**

c. Dialogue Has a Momentum

In real life, if a wife has a list of tasks for her husband, it's not like she stops and arranges them in some kind of a hierarchy. She says whatever is on her mind without striving for some kind of emotional impact. Dialogue scenes are built to arc. That means that the conversations start slowly and then build through conflict, until, at

---

5 GGR, New Line Cinema, Zupnik Cinema Group II, 1992, screenplay by David Mamet

the end of the scene, a character says, "And *that's* why I'm leaving you!" And then we cut to her consulting a divorce attorney. A good dialogue-based scene packs suspense as effectively as the story it is serving does so.

d. Dialogue as a Voice of Authority

One of the most tedious things about modern life is the multiplicity of words that come at us through the media, most of which tell us nothing. As Dostoyevsky notes in his classic work *The Brothers Karamazov*, one of the strongest drives in human nature is the pursuit of a person to trust. Men are basically fearful, and they long to fix their lot in the hands of someone who speaks truth to them without obfuscation or equivocation.

It is one of the appeals of great dialogue that characters speak truth and wisdom in a voice of authority. Characters often "put themselves out there" in dialogue in a way that few real people are wont to do. Indeed, unlike the calculating and über-parsed words of so many of our civic leaders today, a character who continually tells us nothing is generally the butt of the project — nearly always receiving derision and contempt.

One of the things that makes characters appealing is that they are passionate beings, much more passionate than normal people can afford to be on a daily basis. It is the characters' passions that are going to get them in trouble, but also going to draw us to them as sheep in search of the shepherd. The challenge of dialogue is to have characters express their passions delightfully, clearly, and compellingly, but without being "on the nose" and banal.

We love, love, love when characters put themselves out there and speak the truth in a memorable way.

(From *Casablanca*[6])

>   RICK
> The problems of three little people
> don't amount to a hill of beans in this
> old world.

(From *Gone With the Wind*[7])

>   MELANIE
> The happiest days are when babies come.

(From *A Man for All Seasons*[8])

>   THOMAS
> If we lived in a state where virtue
> was profitable, common sense would
> make us saintly. But since we see that
> abhorrence, anger, pride, and stupidity
> commonly profit far beyond charity,
> modesty, justice, and thought, perhaps
> we must stand fast a little — even at
> the risk of being heroes.

e. Dialogue Utilizes Metaphors

Metaphors are teaching tools. The biggest virtue of a metaphor is that it can be clearer than the truth that you are trying to explicate. Teachers struggle to come up with great metaphors to help their students digest complex ideas. One of the great appeals of good dialogue occurs when characters weave perfect metaphors right into their speech. It's the kind of thing you would think of three weeks later in the shower and wish you could go back to slip brilliantly into a conversation.

---

[6] Warner Bros., 1942, screenplay by Julius J. Epstein and Philip G. Epstein and Howard Koch

[7] Warner Bros., 1939, screenplay by Sidney Howard

[8] Highland Films, 1966, screenplay by Robert Bolt

(From *Jerry Maguire*[9])

```
                    JERRY
        Do you want this jacket? I don't need
        it. I'm cloaked in failure!
```

(From *Conspiracy Theory*[10])

```
                    ALICE
        That guy's a restraining order waiting
        to happen.
```

One of the most famous metaphors in a dialogue sequence occurs in Billy Wilder's classic and stylized film noir masterpiece *Double Indemnity*[11]. In this scene, Walter, played by Fred MacMurray, is just starting to hit on the married Phyllis, played by Barbara Stanwyck. He's trying to see if she's game for an affair, and she's thrusting his lines back at him just enough to keep them coming.

```
                    WALTER
        Suppose you get down off your motorcycle
        and give me a ticket?

                    PHYLLIS
        Suppose I let you off with a warning
        this time?

                    WALTER
        Suppose it doesn't take?
```

Notice again the patterns of repetition: "Suppose I..." "suppose I," "suppose you." This brings together two qualities of great dialogue to make the scene delightful to the ear, memorable, and a lot of fun for the actors to play.

---

[9] TriStar Pictures, Gracie Films, 1996, screenplay by Cameron Crowe
[10] Warner Bros., Silver Pictures, 1997, screenplay by Brian Helgeland
[11] Paramount Pictures, 1944, screenplay by Billy Wilder and Raymond Chandler

f. Dialogue Utilizes Subtext

It has been said that people will talk about anything except the elephant sitting in the middle of the room. People don't discuss obvious problems or issues because they find them overwhelming, or they don't have the courage, or they don't have the emotional vocabulary.

If real people avoid saying what they are truly feeling, how much more revealing should dramatic characters be?

Dialogue should reveal character psychology; and very unlike real speech, ooze with all the inner conflicts that are tearing at the characters. When the characters are in the grip of their key struggle, it will be nearly impossible for them to express exactly why they are suffering and / or making the same habitually poor choices. If they do finally say something painfully true, it should come out as an exclamation, vomited into the room like a volcanic eruption.

Some of the greatest humor in screenplays can come from characters talking around their wants and needs because, for a reason the audience intuits, they just can't say the obvious truth.

What are the different subtexts of the following lines of dialogue? What are they telling you about the character in each case?

(From *The Philadelphia Story*[12])

```
                DEXTER
    I thought all writers drank to excess
    and beat their wives. You know, at one
    time I secretly wanted to be a writer.
```

(From *Jurassic Park*[13])

```
                IAN
    I'm always on the lookout for the next
    ex-Mrs. Malcolm.
```

---

[12] Metro-Goldwyn-Mayer, 1940, screenplay by Donald Ogden Stewart
[13] Universal Pictures, Amblin Entertainment, 1993, screenplay by Michael Crichton and David Koepp

(That scene in *When Harry Met Sally...*[14])

<pre>
           LADY IN CAFÉ
   I'll have what she's having.
</pre>

g. Dialogue Exists to Process Conflict

> *I write plays because writing dialogue is the only respectable*
> *way of contradicting yourself. I put in a position, rebut*
> *it, refute the rebuttal, and rebut the refutation.*
>
> — TOM STOPPARD

In real life, we talk to each other to give each other information. In drama, characters communicate to process conflict. A dialogue scene needs to very consciously be a tug of war. There needs to be overt agendas and subtextual ones. It's all a battle played out in pithy and delightful language.

Death by Verbal Cliché

The difference between a "B" script and an "A" script very often comes down to how many trite platitudes or euphemisms the writer allows into his work. Most of these are so hackneyed that they elicit laughter from readers. Save your work the disdain, and take the pledge never to use any of these:

1. "Look, [anything]."
2. "You mean..." (fearfully asked, half-spoken reiteration of something obvious)
3. "You look as if you've seen a ghost."
4. "This is not about [whatever]. It's about [whatever]."
5. "We gotta get outta here!"
6. "I'm only gonna say this one time..." (said for the gazillionth time in history)
7. "Why you're... you're trembling." (spoken by a swain just about to kiss a girl)

---

[14] Castle Rock Entertainment, Nelson Entertainment, 1989, screenplay by Nora Ephron

8. "That can mean only one thing..." (which the viewers have already figured out)

9. "She's been living a lie." (which is obvious to everybody)

10. "Don't blame yourself." (to someone who is doing just that)

11. "Oh, you shouldn't have!" (said by a girl who has just gotten a gift)

12. "Everybody has their price." (said by someone trying to buy somebody else off)

13. "You have to move on with your life."

14. "Are you thinking what I'm thinking?" (Well, I'm thinking that you are derivative.)

15. "I just need some help getting back on my feet..."

16. "Who do you think you are?" (said by an insecure, smarmy person to the hero)

17. "Who do you think you're talking to?" (said by an insecure, smarmy person)

18. "I was born ready."

19. "Don't you die on me!"

20. "I'll show you." (said by an angry, down-on-his-luck person to someone better off)

21. "What part of _____ don't you understand?"

22. "No way! I'm coming with you!"

23. "What is it? You can tell me."

24. "How could you do this to me?"

25. "Don't let your dreams die."

26. "You go, girl!"

27. "I can't believe this is happening."

28. "I don't wanna know."

29. "If I've said it once, I've said it a hundred times..." (Yeah, we've heard it too.)

30. "I thought you were my friend."

31. "Nothing can change the way I feel about you." (except maybe your use of trite phrases)

32. "Why do I feel like I've known you my whole life?" (Because I speak in platitudes?)

33. "No matter what tomorrow may bring..."

34. "Forget me. I'm no good for you."

35. "How many times do I have to say it?" (Never again would be fine.)

36. "I can explain! This isn't what it looks like!"

37. "Don't lie to me."

38. "We're / You're / He's never going to make it!"

39. "Is that all you got?"

40. "_____ is my middle name."

41. "He's standing right behind me, isn't he?"

42. "I'm getting too old for this s#!t." (said by a harried lawyer / police chief / anyone)

h. Dialogue-Writing Tips and Exercises

- **If it can be shown visually, do that instead.** Use dialogue sparingly. Instead, find more visual and active ways to reveal your character's wants and needs. Rather than have a character talk about what a great football player he is, show him tackling his opponent.

- **Answer a question with a question.** Find ways for your characters to reveal more subtext. Often, the best way to do this is to never let them have all the information they need. Answering a question with a question is a good way to create tension and make dialogue more interesting.

Example:

BOB	BOB
Why are you here?	Why are you here?
SALLY	SALLY
I'm doing my laundry.	Why are you always getting on my case?

```
        BOB                    BOB
    Oh.                    Why do you always
                           have to be like that?
```

- **Never let your characters say what's on their mind when subtext will do.** The purpose of dialogue is to heighten tension in a scene.

- **If you let them say what's on their mind, let them go farther than anyone dare would in real life.** In writing dramas or even some comedies, characters need to vent some hard truths to another character. The dam breaks, and everything the character has been withholding comes out. These scenes are typically earned after many previous encounters that were all subtext. Often these scenes reveal what an audience's thoughts about a character have been all along.

- **Don't write complete sentences.** Dialogue is almost never grammatically correct, unless one is writing lines for the Duchess of Grantham. It is most often concise sentence fragments grouped together in a rhythmic fashion.

- **Avoid fillers and intro words.** Words like *yeah, um, look, well,* and *maybe* should be cut. Sometimes actors will add these words, but avoid them in original drafts.

- **Be very specific.** Great writing, especially comedy writing, is dependent on specific, visual references. If you have a character say, "You're a terrible person," that's not nearly as interesting as having the character say, "Satan must love having you as his lapdog."

- **Rephrase your rhetoric.** Great writers continuously find better ways to phrase their dialogue. Sometimes it means changing the order of the words around, and sometimes it means finding more colorful words.

- **Avoid exposition.** We've all seen those scenes in which a character spews out all the facts of what just happened to catch another character up to speed. Sometimes exposition is unavoidable; but in most cases, there are better ways to get information across.

- **Avoid the characters' names.** Unless characters are meeting for the first time, this is usually unnecessary.
- **Avoid verbal clichés.** Clichés are all the things we've heard a million times before, such as the phrase, "a million times before." Clichés are bad because they make the audience tune out. Transform your clichés into more original ideas.

CHAPTER 7

NOTES ON THEME:
THE GOOD, THE GREAT, AND THE UGLY

THE NOTES:

- **"What is this supposed to be about?"**
- **"The story felt like it had no spine."**
- **"Why should I care what happened 600 years ago?"**
- **"Very unsatisfying at the end."**

In *The Poetics*, Aristotle lists "theme" as the third most crucial element to a dramatic story. Confusion about the nature of theme wrecks many screenplays, because it is a key element that serves to organize the whole telling — especially of your B-story, which is your main character's inner journey. If you don't have a good grasp of your theme, you won't really know where your act breaks need to fall, and when your story is really over.

> *The peculiar quality of the "joy" in successful story can thus be*
> *explained as a sudden glimpse of the underlying reality or truth.*
> *It is not only a "consolation" for the sorrow of this world, but*
> *a satisfaction, and an answer to that question, "Is it true?"*
> —J. R. R. TOLKIEN

The theme in a story is the writer's underlying presupposition about humanity and the world that raises the relating of events into an organized sum of many parts. It is the theme that gives a story its resonance and meaning. The whole project gets organized around the theme — particularly the structure, the tone, the visual and production style, and, of course, the actors' performances.

Generally, a writer needs to have an idea of theme before starting to write. Invariably, as the story grows, the theme morphs too; or, more likely, an entirely new theme starts to appear. It's actually hard to know what a story ultimately means until it is done being told, but a writer needs to have some idea for a project to get out of the starting gate.

a. Theme Is a Thesis

A theme is a thesis that can be argued. A good theme is a *true* thesis that can be argued. A great theme is a true thesis that people urgently want to argue.

A "thesis that can be argued" means that a story is ultimately an expression of a writer's point of view about the world. On the level of theme, story is basically a demonstration of something that a writer believes to be true about the world. The story plays out as though the writer were saying, "Here's what I think." Consequently, to be successful, the writer needs to have the wherewithal to actually have thoughts about things, and then the courage to put his or her thoughts out there.

A theme can still work as the project's organizing principle, even if it is objectively untrue. An example of this is a movie like *Million Dollar Baby*. The theme of the movie is something to the effect of: "A good coach is someone who pushes past all his boundaries to be there for his trainee." In the movie, this notion manifests itself at the end as the coach, played by Clint Eastwood, euthanizes his seriously wounded trainee because she has lost her hope in life. The suggestion is that killing one's student is just one more thing that a coach needs to do sometimes.

This theme is erroneous and hugely problematic from a moral standpoint. The end result of an untrue theme is that the audience walks away with a sense of disquiet. The story just doesn't sit well, and very often the memory of the movie will evoke discomfort. This isn't the kind of emotion that leads people to repeat viewings or good word of mouth. In the end, you can't sell a lie.

A "thesis that people want to argue" indicates that your story is tapping into the zeitgeist of a particular cultural moment. Your movie is about a topic that is flowing in and around what is being said at the water coolers.

An example of a good theme is: "Creativity and friendship have a symbiotic relationship." This thesis suggests that you can't have good art without some kind of supportive human relationship. This is going to be a movie that challenges the "loner artist" notion, and instead advances the vision that art is somehow related to community. This theme should produce an intriguing and compelling story that will have a shelf life as long as there are artists among men. But it is probably not going to seize the attention of the nation or the globe.

An example of a great theme for the early twenty-first century is present in *The Hunger Games*. The theme of this highly successful story franchise is: "When the whole world has lost its mind, you can retain your sanity through love." Supporting themes in *The Hunger Games* which also capture today's zeitgeist include: "A celebrity culture devolves into oppression" and "People can to a large extent be controlled through poverty." The astounding success of *The Hunger Games* comes from the fact that all of these themes are floating around in the back of everyone's minds at this cultural moment. In a society without leaders or a new frontier, dystopian literature is back and hot.

If a theme is the organizing principle of a story, than a project with no theme or a bad theme is going to be disorganized and lacking a fundamental cohesion.

A bad theme is an obvious or undeveloped idea.

People are drawn to stories instinctually, as Aristotle noted, because they are beings who seek to know. As we noted earlier, the success of a story in satisfying this "instinct for imitation" depends upon its depth of insight. If a movie is built around an idea that is obvious, then the audience will feel cheated at the end. You had two hours of their time, but you gave them something they knew walking in. Examples of bad themes in this sense are "murder is bad" or "people mean more than stuff" or the utterly overdone and unhelpful background notion of so many Gen X movie projects, "life is unfair."

Another poor choice is to substitute amorphous, meandering brooding with no real point-of-view risk to actually make any sort of statement for an actual theme. This is a writer saying, "My script's theme is jealousy" or "my theme is motherhood." The rejoinder to this is, "What about motherhood? What do you have to say about it?"

The problem with a one-word theme is that it doesn't provide the direction and organizing principle that themes should. It also means that the project will feel cheap to the viewer, as though the writer didn't deliver on his or her contract with the audience.

b. Exercises to Strengthen Your Theme

1. Put your theme into a thesis statement. Is it arguable? Is it too obvious? Is it something that people will want to talk about? If not, go deeper into your character's transformational arc and make his inner paradox more compelling. (For example, when you stand back from your story and consider your theme, if you get, "Dads need to learn that family is more important than career," then you have an obvious theme. Push into why your character is pursuing career and ignoring family. What is really driving him? Maybe your theme could be written more accurately as, "Men put career before family because career is easier." That would be something over which people could argue.)

2. Write out a statement which is the antithesis of your theme. That is, write out the opposite argument from the one that your story seems to be making. Imagine how the story would change if you were developing this antithesis. What weaknesses does this reveal in the way you are developing your theme?

3. Find a metaphorical device or image that you can you create in your story to explicate and demonstrate your theme. (For example, in Ang Lee's movie *The Ice Storm*, the literal ice storm outside was a metaphor for the effects of the Sexual Revolution in the families being portrayed. Instead of being warming, the sex in the story was chilling and even death-dealing.)

CHAPTER 8

NOTES ON TONE AND GENRE:

GETTING ON THE SAME PAGE

THE NOTES:

- "This felt like two different movies."
- "It's all "ha-ha!" funny, and then there's a murder-suicide."
- "Who is the audience for this piece?"
- "What do you want us to feel here?"

a. Genre Is What We Feel

Genre literally means "type" in Greek. What type of story do you want to tell? Type is very important. It informs the marketers and distributors how to sell your movie. It also informs your audience what they are watching.

People go to the movies to *feel* something. The best way to choose a genre for your story is to think about the emotions of the piece. What is the primary emotion that you want your audience to feel when watching your movie? What is the physical reaction you want to elicit from your audience? Do you want them to laugh or cry?

There are three meta-genres: drama, comedy, and horror. All stories fit under one of these meta-genre headings based upon the primary emotion it elicits from the audience. The sign that a story is successful is that it leads the audience to experience a physical response appropriate to the project's genre.

Drama — People watch dramas to experience pathos and sympathy. The primary emotion needed for drama is sadness. The intended physical response from the audience is tears.

Comedy — People watch comedies to experience surprise and the absurd. The primary emotion that needs to be generated in a comedy is joy. The intended physical response is laughter.

Horror — People watch horror films to experience the limits of their own courage. The primary emotion that storytellers need to create in a horror film is fear. The intended physical response is bodily tension, which may be released through a scream or sweating or ducking or squeezing one's eyes shut or gripping the arm of a chair.

Many novice screenwriters, when asked about genre, tell us that their stories don't have one, or that they have a mixed one. That's like saying your bowl of ice cream doesn't have a flavor, or that the flavor is vanilla pickle. Genres should be pure. Popular today is genre blending, such as the dramedy. This is when there are two primary emotions vying for equal space in the story and eliciting an equal number of physical responses. There are few films that actually pull off blended genres well. Many end up being confused genres instead of blended ones. We recommend first mastering one type of genre before attempting to blend two of them.

Now, of course there are many more emotions to feel in a story, and there are many more types of stories out there. We call these subgenres. There are many of them, but they all fall within the comedy, drama, or horror meta-genres, imbued by an added nuance that makes them their own.

Here is a partial list of subgenres, their primary emotion, and their intended audience response.

Subgenre	Emotion	Response
Action	Thrill / Tension	"Whew!"
Adventure	Excitement	"Wow!"
Western	Outrage at injustice	"That's not right."
Romance	Love / Angst	"Awww."
Sci-Fi	Worry	"Uh-oh. This won't end well."
Fantasy	Wonder	"Cool."

There are also genres for the audience it is intended to serve. These are genres like "family," "Christian," "gay and lesbian," et cetera. These are "niche" audiences in which the story is intended to affirm a particular belief or lifestyle. The problem with these categories as subgenres, however, is that they can seem agenda-driven or heavy-handed if they make their intended message more important than the intended emotion or audience response. Many of these movies seem to be designed to merely compel the audience to ask, "Hey, aren't we [the members of this clique] great?" rather than eliciting a true core emotion, like joy or fear. It is all the more important for niche genres to find something authentic to say about life and human nature by getting to a core emotion. If you are working within one of these niche meta-genres, it is even more crucial that you tell a masterful story.

b. Tone Is the Rhythm of Your Story

While genre is pure, tone can be mixed. Tone is the way your genre will be played out. If you are writing a horror film, the tone informs whether it will be terrifying and realistic like *The Exorcist*; gruesome and gratuitous like *Saw*; or funny and ridiculous like *Scary Movie*. It is the difference between the *Batman* of the 1960s (colorful) and the *Batman* of the 2000s (dark).

We find that tone is often overlooked in screenplay drafts. The way a draft is written, even in the action lines, is largely dependent on tone. If it's a fast-paced action movie, the "read" of the draft should also be fast-paced, using fewer words and more white space on the page.

To best understand tone in a story, treat a project as if it were a piece of music. Tone in music is a combination of three elements: pitch, volume, and quality.

1. **Pitch** refers to the frequency of vibrations in a musical note or piece. Many sound vibrations in a short period will create a pitch that is high. Similarly, in storytelling, tone is very much a matter of how fast the story beats are coming. In an adventure story or a comedy, the beats are coming machine-gun fast. The movie story is moving and changing rapidly, with nearly one beat on every page of script.

   In a drama, where pathos is the goal, there are many fewer beats, and the audience has the opportunity to dwell on them for much longer periods.

2. **Volume** in music simply means how loud the notes are being played. Are they being banged out like a jackhammer, or are they coming soft as rain?

   In a similar way, in a story, the beats may be very violent, making a visceral change in arena or character (as in action movies); or they may be very subtle and nuanced (as in certain dramas).

3. Quality in music refers to the power of combining certain musical ideas to evoke different emotions. Certain musicians or composers might be better equipped to play on or write the scores of particular film genres.

   So, in storytelling, tone can be secured through subtle nuances in language and writing style. A writer needs to strategize ways of crafting a script that will elicit and heighten the desired emotions of a piece.

c. Tone and Genre Exercises

1. Hand out a scene from your movie to two or three readers. Observe them reading your piece. Do they laugh or bite their lip? Do they yawn or do they make comments about the subject

at hand? What emotions if any did your pages elicit? Figure out what in your writing got a response, and how to heighten those emotions.

2. In thriller, horror, or suspense stories, experiment with making the point of view more limited or unreliable. How does your story change and grow in tension when you tell it through the eyes of a child? Or of a simpleton? Or of an unstable person?

3. In comedy, write out five absurd situations in which to place your character. How can you make these even more absurd? How can you add a surprising payoff to each of these moments?

4. Count the beats in your first act. This is the pitch of your story. Do you have enough for the genre you are working in? Do you have too many?

5. Consider the volume of your beats. Are they too subtle for the genre? Too intense?

6. What flourishes can you add to your story to heighten the genre and tone? Try using more colorful and textural words to describe locations. Try making the external environment a complement to the action of the story. Try making the style of the character's speech mirror a better complement to the tone.

CHAPTER 9

SPECTACLE AS THE SERVANT OF ALL

THE NOTES:

- **"Not enough is happening in this story."**
- **"Can we get a car chase in here?"**
- **"Too many explosions!"**
- **"Is there something to look at in this story?"**
- **"Where's the sizzle?"**

From the early days of the movies, an aspect of the visual storytelling experience has been what film historian Tom Gunning calls the "Cinema of Attractions." That means that part of the audience's expectations in a dramatic production is going to be seeing something they haven't seen before. "Spectacle" is the last and least important listing on the hierarchy of six essential story elements in Aristotle's *The Poetics*. Sorry, Michael Bay.

Spectacle is necessary, but it is the most humble of the elements in story because it serves all the others (and is not served by any other).

"Spectacle" in a movie story is the answer to the question, "What is fun for the audience in this project?" Aristotle notes that "fun" in drama basically means evoking strong and worthy emotions. He says that in drama, the audience will love you more if you make them suffer more through dramatic pain.

Thinking of spectacle as the element that serves all the other elements is helpful because it means that real spectacle will never function independently of the other elements. There need to be elements of spectacle in all of the other elements, but spectacle serving itself ends up feeling empty and cheap.

This is the indictment that so many people throw at the movies since the blockbuster era began: "That movie is nothing but special effects with no heart or meaning." People know instinctively when the hierarchy or story elements have been violated.

A writer should ask himself, "What is the spectacle in my plot?" That is, what is going to be the fun part for the audience in the plot itself? Generally, the fun in the plot involves the cleverness of the twists and reversals, the details of the arena, and the key emotional moments of the story.

Again, attention needs to be given to spectacle in the character. This might mean the quirky quality that separates this character from all others, the thing she can do, or some intriguing and distinct aspect of her style.

Spectacle in theme might mean the use of visual imagery and metaphor to serve the theme, or the structural device that leads to the reveal thereof. The spectacle may be in the point-of-view device through which the story is told. Or it could be the process scenes involved in the arena. Remember the Woody repair and makeover scene in *Toy Story*? Remember the barn-raising sequence in *Witness*? People love process sequences, for they generally have something to teach.

Don't think of spectacle as the "icing" on the story "cake." It isn't; it's either the excellence and "something extra" in every part of the cake, or it's derailing your story.

a. Spectacle Exercise

Make a list of each of the main categories of elements in your story. Opposite from each element, write the spectacle that will make that element entertaining for the audience. It should look something like the following:

STORY ELEMENTS	SPECTACLE
A) Plot	Inciting incident comes out of the character's own folly. Reversals are each an echo of the character's four life goals.
B) Character	Character sees all his friends as characters from *The Jungle Book*.
C) Arena	Takes place on an army base in Taiwan during monsoon season.
D) Dialogue	The main character speaks bad Chinese, which the audience sees via subtitles.
E) Theme	Represented by the symbols of the character's family crest.
F) Cinematic Quality	Lots of visual exploration of Chinese-language character symbols.
G) Structure	Told as cutaways during a climactic real-time martial-arts contest.

CHAPTER 10

STRUCTURE NOTES:
HOW YOU REVEAL THE PLOT

THE NOTES:

- "Nothing happens until page 35."
- "Too much going on here! Let us catch a breath!"
- "Not enough rollercoaster in this story."
- "Act Two drags."
- "The ending isn't satisfying enough."
- "Too many red herrings."
- "Not enough setup in the first act."
- "Setups weren't paid off in the third act."
- "Too much exposition."

As it was in the days of Aristotle and later Shakespeare, most full-length stage or screen dramas still consist of three acts. Even when the project is not full length, as in a short film, the story still needs to have a beginning, middle, and end with all the beats knit together in a relationship of necessity.

Acts are composed of scenes that showcase turning points in the narrative. A turning point is a screen moment that advances the story, foreshadows a coming crisis or resolution, or gives important information about the main character. The best scenes do all three.

There are many theories about where the principal turning points in a screenplay need to occur. A good rule for new writers is to be sure that every page of your screenplay brings with it some kind of turning point. Every scene also needs to have a beginning, middle, and end according to the dramatic point of that screen moment. After completing the first draft of your piece, go back and try lifting every scene out. If the piece still works without that scene, then either get rid of it, or rewrite it to be a more dramatic event.

a. Act One: The Beginning

Act One is the most complex part of the story because you have so much to do in so little time. Act One should run about thirty pages, and the following needs to be accomplished:

- **Set the tone for the piece.** If it is a comedy, people need to be laughing in the first few minutes, and then all through the first act. If it is a thriller, generally, somebody needs to die so that the project launches with suspense. If it is a drama, we need to feel a loss early on. Beyond genre, the first act is the place where you lay out the style of the whole piece. Is this highly stylized art? Is it gritty realism? Is it "through the eyes of a child," or using some other kind of narration? Is it told in a linear way or in flashbacks? All of this needs to be introduced in the beginning.

- **Introduce the main character.** You have to develop a bond between the character and the viewer by showing off your character as sympathetic, potentially heroic, or compelling in some way. You have to hint at the character's fatal flaw — which could lead to his destruction.

- **Introduce the supporting characters — friends, villains, and mentors.** You have to situate your main character in his world, and allow the viewer to learn the "rules" of that world. The first few minutes of a story is when the audience is doing the most brain work, tracking characters and absorbing story information. Be careful not to spend too much time on information and characters that aren't necessary to the advancement of the story. Also, the conventional industry wisdom is that an audience can track the transformational arc of no more than seven characters at a time. Limit the amount of characters you are introducing right away.

- **Establish the main conflict.** By page 10, the viewer should know what this story is about. What is the main conflict in which the characters are going to be swept up? This conflict has to be engaging for the viewer such that he will feel something is at stake, along with the principal characters. Generally, Act One ends with a major turning point in the life of the main character. He or she makes a significant change or comes to a devastating realization.

- **Two or three beats** and turning points need to happen in the first act. In a feature, generally, one happens on page ten. The other happens on page thirty. These beats should be visual, high-stakes, and irrevocable, meaning they can't be undone.

- **Introduce the theme** through some kind of visual imagery or device.

- **Set up the viewer.** Act One should be a series of hints and clues. Lots of barely noticeable details that will all come together in the resolution of the piece in Act Three. You need to cleverly weave in important facts about every character, including their backgrounds, aptitudes, experiences, habits, what they carry around in their pockets, what color underwear they put on that morning — anything that can be exploited to resolve the work at the end. Be wary of sowing too many red herrings. They can annoy and frustrate your viewer. You don't want to do that.

b. Act Two: The Middle

Act Two is the longest act in a drama. In a screenplay, it should run about 60 pages. In Act Two, you need to accomplish the following:

- **Complicate all of the conflicts introduced in Act One.** Make them much worse than they at first seemed.
- **Flesh out the main character** by showing the viewer how the character's fatal flaw trips him up over and over. Prepare the viewer for the coming climactic struggle by confirming to them that this character could go either way.
- **Flesh out the villain** or adversary by showing his power and advantages in moment after moment. The villain clearly has the upper hand in Act Two.
- **Provide a few delightful moments of cinematic enjoyment.** Let the viewer exhale — hopefully with a laugh. There are often sequences where the main character explores the new world or the circumstances that brought him into Act Two.
- **Set up some reversals.** Reversals are unexpected plot twists, and Act Two is a great place to use some. Does a mentor turn out to be a villain? Does a villain have a soft spot? Does your main character switch tactics? Reversals can also indicate growth or change for a character, which can further the plot.
- **Set up the main climax of the piece.** By the end of Act Two, the viewer should feel that there is only the slimmest chance that the hero will save his soul or the whole world. He is close to giving up.
- **Let there be death.** The end of Act Two is often signaled by an "all hope is lost" moment, or death of some kind, whether it is a plan, a dream, or a character. Act Three then becomes about rebuilding from that death.

c. Act Three: The End

Act Three should run about 30 pages. A good ending provides the audience with resolution, satisfaction, and scope for the imagination.

"Resolution" means that the action of the story has come to an end. All the questions posed in the journey of the story have been answered.

"Satisfaction" means that all the resolutions have been clever and delightful.

"Scope for the imagination" means that the viewer often reflects on the characters in the piece, and wonders about their next chapter. In that sense, a great ending always feels like a new beginning to the audience.

In Act Three, you have to accomplish the following:

- **Accelerate suspense to a fever pitch.** Your character is fully engaged in the conflict. He calls all his resources into play.
- **The character is presented with a high-stakes moment of grace.** It will often take the form of a sacrifice that unifies the whole journey of the story and means an irrevocable change in his or her life.
- **Resolution.** The main character beats the odds, turns the tables on his foes, and achieves self-fulfillment (unless it's a tragedy). You can't accomplish this by bringing in any new facts about the character or situation. The resolution is completely tied to your promise to...
- **Pay off all your setups.** All the hints and clues you seeded into Act One bloom into integral story elements in Act Three.
- **Get out fast.** Once you've resolved the story, don't hang around. Fade out.

d. The Beauty of the Beat

In a story, a beat is a change in the action. If story is a long chain of little dots connected together, then a beat is one of those little dots.

Scenes are written around beats. There should be at least one beat in every scene. If a scene doesn't have a change in the action of the story, we generally ask why it is there in the first place. Beat-less scenes can generally be lopped out without the screenplay missing them at all.

Beats are not conversations. They can cause conversations. They can be talked over and before and after, but a beat is not talk. It is action.

One indication that a story is in trouble occurs when a writer completes a "beat sheet" — that is, a chronological list of all the actions in a story — and a quarter of the "beats" are conversations. We always go through and cross all of these out, and tell the writer to go back and make something happen that the characters can talk about.

A beat is the action that it is the *raison d'être* of the scene. It is the center of the scene that provides all the energy and the life of the story. In a very real way, we call them beats because they are the pulse or heartbeats of the script.

The best beats come out of conflict. This means that a character is continually propelled into action by the complications arising from his prior choices. One choice causes tension, which leads to another choice, and so on. Conflict can be heightened in dialogue, and so the beat can be seen as the culmination of the dialogue scene.

A reversal is a beat that is unexpected and takes the story into an unforeseen direction. It's more than just an action. It's a surprise. Aristotle noted that the best stories are full of reversals, what he called "complex stories." They require the audience to sit up and be attentive lest they get lost as the story moves along. A "simple story," by contrast, still has beats, but they are plodding one after the other without any twists and turns.

An example of a simple story would be one in which a man is dying of cancer. He gets diagnosed in Act One; he and his family suffer and adjust in Act Two; and then he dies in Act Three. The delight in the story will be in the emotions of the characters; and the beats will be the step-by-step progression of the disease and its consequences.

A complex plot with a similar story might also involve a man dying of cancer. He also gets diagnosed in Act One, but then a reversal might be that while his family focuses on his disease in Act Two, his wife suddenly dies of a stroke. That would be a beat which is a reversal. Then, in Act Three, the character doesn't die, but maybe has to live without the love of his life.

Both stories would have beats; but in one story they would be in a straight line, and in the other they would not be.

e. Scene Structure: The Building Blocks of Your Story

Beats are contained in scenes. While beats are the moments that drive the action of a story forward, the scene is what brings the story as a whole to life. Beats are skeletons; scenes are flesh, blood, and skin.

Every scene in a screenplay is like its own mini-movie. Each scene in a movie has parts that contribute to the whole of the film, just like every cell in our body contains our DNA. In addition to the beat, which forwards the plot, new information should be revealed about every other part of the story through plot, character, theme, dialogue, music, and spectacle.

Most writers can only focus on plot, character, and maybe some theme when writing first drafts, so it is imperative to go through each scene looking to pull out the other elements during revisions. When combing through scenes in the rewrite process, the mantra should be, "Nothing missing, nothing extra."

Plot

The plot must move forward in some way in every scene. It can be the main plot, or the subplot — but ideally both. If you have a scene that does not move the story forward, it is not essential to the story and should be cut or combined with another scene.

Character

Every active choice a character makes should be revealing, propelling individual scenes and the larger story forward. In a scene, plot and character work together to convey vital information. Every scene should reveal character in some way. Minimally, it reveals important information about the main characters in the scene. Ideally, it reveals character from every person in the scene.

Theme

Every scene in a movie should be consistent with the overall theme of the story. That means looking at the content of each scene and asking, "Is this really what I want to say?" Theme can be enhanced through imagery, sound, dialogue, et cetera.

Dialogue

Not every scene needs to have actual dialogue, but there should be some consideration as to what is being communicated. Is the central question of the story moving forward and developing? If there is dialogue in the scene, does the information convey plot and reveal character, or is it just fun, extra stuff? (Extra stuff is not allowed.)

Music

Music, including sound design, is often overlooked, but it is integral to screen storytelling. Pulling sound through the scene will enhance the tone and the theme, and can even help further the plot. While sound is absolutely necessary, a word of caution in using songs with lyrics: They can distract from the story if they are not the central focus of the moment. Some stories successfully incorporate lyrics into the narrative, such as a few choice Beatles lyrics in *I Am Sam*. The lyrics worked in that movie because they were central to the theme and the development of characters. Lyrics should not, however, be shortcuts for dialogue (unless the film is a musical). Also, if writing a low-budget movie, take care not to include music that could blow the production budget obtaining licensing rights.

Spectacle

Just like the overall story, each scene should have something that entertains or delights the audience. While the "big" spectacle moments are structured around the turning points, each scene should be engaging in some way and contribute to the rollercoaster-like ride of the story. Spectacle can be embedded in plot, character, theme, dialogue, or sound.

f. Structure Exercises

1. List the principal conflicts that you will be bringing out in your story. In a few sentences write the beginning, middle, and end of each conflict.

2. Make a list of all the sub-stories in your story and title them "A Story," "B Story," "C Story," "D Story," et cetera. Under each title, list the main beats of each story and the scenes in which those beats occur. You should be able to see the beginning, middle, and end of each story. Ask yourself which of the stories need more attention, conflict, and resolution.

3. Create a blended outline of your story by dividing the various story beats across the three acts. This will help you know which stories you need to serve in each scene. Below is an example to get you started. Your actual blended outline will cover all three acts.

BLENDED OUTLINE

ACT ONE

Scene One — A Story, C Story

Scene Two — A Story, B Story, E Story

Scene Three — A Story

Scene Four — D Story, E Story

Scene Five — A Story, B Story, E Story

Scene Six — A Story, C Story

Scene Seven — A Story, B Story, D Story

ACT TWO

Scene Eight — E Story

Scene Nine — A Story, B Story

Scene Ten — A Story, C Story, D Story

CHAPTER 11

CINEMATIC NOTES:
DOES IT HAVE TO BE A MOVIE?

THE NOTES:

- "This felt like it wanted to be a novel."
- "It's all talk with nothing to see."
- "This movie is a painful slog."
- "All the cinematic techniques get in the way of the story."

So many notes could die before they are even born in a reader's brain, if only the screenwriter loved movies more. In the same way that we said writers need to be readers, movie writers need to be watchers. They need to be students of the cinematic art form so that they grow in respect of the limits and possibilities afforded by the medium. A lot of writers are simply thinking too small, like a painter who has twenty colors on his palette but chooses to use only yellow. It's one thing if a talented master uses only one color to explore its potential. It's quite another thing when a beginner confines herself to one color because she has no idea other hues exist.

Many books have been written about the nature of "film form" and the myriad techniques that cinema offers storytellers. Virginia Woolf noted wryly that it would never be possible to offer a pure criticism of a film akin to the criticism applied to music or a painting, because, knitted as it is to technology, the art form of cinema is always in flux. Still, scriptwriters need to always be asking themselves, "Why does my story need to be a movie?" That is, what am I doing with this tale such that only the possibilities of cinema can do it justice?

The word "cinema" goes back to the very beginning of the art form. It is short for the name of the first projection machine, which was called a *cinematograph*, from the Greek words for "moving" and "pictures." With the introduction of sound into cinema, the art form expanded; and then, with the revolution of sound technology, it became downright misleading to think of what we watch on the screen as mere moving pictures. Still, the word *cinema* helps us because it does explain the key element of this art form: movement. As people in Hollywood are wont to say, "Movies move." Their images are flashing by; their sounds are rising and falling while the score is flowing in between everything, filling in all the cracks; their stories are about visual choices; their hearts are characters on an inner journey to wisdom while climbing some external mountain.

A truly cinematic story is one that moves in terms of content and method through the harmonization of a multiplicity of art forms. See Appendix A for a list of some of the most influential movies ever made, all of which display masterful cinematic craft and storytelling.

Here are the defining qualities of cinema. A writer must take advantage of them if his or her project is going to fully function as a movie.

a. A Movie Is a Harmony of Elements

Creating a movie is very much like writing a symphony. To create a beautiful piece of symphonic music, the composer first needs to master dozens of instruments. Mastery here means that the composer understands the fundamental gift of each instrument — what it brings to the musical table in a way that no other instrument can. The composer, then, needs to work out a "main theme" which is the essence of his piece. He marshals each of the instruments to dance around that theme, to play with it, to bring out its different strains, to bring it fully to life.

Cinema is first and foremost a harmonization of the four principal art forms: composition, music, literature, and theater, which in themselves encompass many other constituent art forms. The person creating a movie needs to revere all of the different "instruments" that go into making a movie.

1. **Composition** refers broadly to the ability to communicate and even move people through the arrangement of visual elements. Included herein are the art forms of visual design, all of which use color, shapes, and shadows as their main tools. Under this heading also fall lighting and photography, production design, location scouting, set decoration, costuming, hair and makeup, animation, and visual effects.

2. **Music** refers to the score of the project, which is meant to unite the whole piece and heighten the emotions of every character. In a broader way, music incorporates all the manufactured sounds that form the auditory part of the cinema experience. Art forms here are sound design, musical composition, and instrumentation; and vocal performance, sound effects, and sound editing.

3. **Literature** refers to the storytelling aspect of cinema. The creation of an entertaining plot, compelling characters, witty or pungent dialogue, a unifying theme, and a sturdy overall structure are all components of the larger art form of storytelling.

4. **Theater** here means staging and performance and drama. Drama as stories meant to be performed according to a certain digestible size and scope. Stories meant to be witnessed, which are played out in front of a group of people whose common experiences are a big part of the art form.

In classical philosophy, "harmony," with wholeness and radiance, is the definition of beauty. Harmony means complementarity. It means that the excellence of the parts of a work of art are measured by how well they mesh with the other parts to make the whole. It's the whole — the sum of the parts, and the reason that they are all being brought together — that matters.

b. Moving Through Time and Place: Transitions

Because cinema is moving, writers need to be conscious of how the screenplay moves the viewer from one place to another along with the characters. If scenes are written correctly, their momentum will leave the characters in not only a different plot place, but probably a different psychological or emotional place as well.

The transition out of one scene and into the next can reflect this. This can be accomplished visually, but also using the soundtrack through music, ambient sound, and dialogue. Cinema can make direct associations across time and space, and from image to meaning in a way impossible in other art forms. Writers who ignore this potential end up with movies that feel draggy and clunky.

Some examples of wonderful transitions in cinema:

- Early in the Oscar-winning film *Babette's Feast*, there is a match cut from the elderly sisters to the young women on the cusp of adulthood they had been forty years earlier. The years dissolve away as the screen blurs, and the audience resets in tandem as the weathered, tired faces become lovely and full of potential.

- In another Oscar-winning film, *Life Is Beautiful*, there is a stunning transition through time and relationship. The hero watches the object of his affections, his "principessa," walk up some stairs into a flower-filled room. After a moment of thought, he follows her. His pause represents the question "Is she the one?" running across the young man's features and in his spirit. He decides to commit, and follows her into the recesses of the bower off camera. A second or two goes by, and then we hear the mature man and woman calling from off screen. Suddenly, a little boy, about four years old, runs out and joins his mother and father — the former young man and his principessa — who have obviously gotten married, settled down, and now have a family. The transition not only whisks us through time, but also makes a statement about what commitment makes possible. It is the coming together of story, character, and theme in a way that only cinema can do.

- An example of powerful sound transition accompanying visual transition in cinema occurs in the comedy *Notting Hill*. Using the song, "Ain't No Sunshine When She's Gone," the movie takes the viewer through nearly a whole year in about two minutes of screen time. While the song plays, we watch the main character travel through the seasons of grief; the literal seasons beat against him as he walks the main street of Notting Hill. Everything around him changes and stays the same while he plods on, nearly unconscious. Finally, as summer unfolds, he raises his head up and smiles. He has begun to come out of his suffering.

c. Layering In the Meaning

Cinema is powerful because it not only packs the power of the four principal art forms, but because it can deliver them simultaneously. Composition, music, literature, and theater come at the viewer all at once, making for an almost overwhelming, uniquely human experience for the senses and mind to unravel. This is why we love the movies.

A screen storyteller needs to become accomplished at delivering information economically in time but lavishly in quantity through the various methods the medium makes possible. Scenes that really work are ones that are advancing in a layered way, fulfilling all the different storytelling tasks.

And what layers of communication are possible in cinema?
- Composition (what we are seeing)
- Lyrical imagery (what we are seeing as metaphors)
- Juxtaposition of images (how what we are seeing is edited together)
- Dialogue, including voiceover and off-screen

- Music and other non-diegetic sound
- Ambient sound

Each of these tools should be given roles throughout the screen story to communicate with the viewer. Many times, the viewer won't even be conscious that they are receiving information, as with ambient sounds (like cars going by outside). The purpose of those sounds is to make the viewer accept that there is a larger world outside which is impacting the characters.

It is the mark of a beginner to do everything one piece at a time. So there will be a few minutes to pan around the arena and show us where we are. Then we will have the main character enter and do something sympathetic. Then the main character will do or say something to tell us what his wants and needs are. Then we meet the antagonist. Et cetera, et cetera.

Cinematic mastery is achieved when the arena unfolds gradually according to the overall structure; characters makes choices that launch the plot and announce their wants and needs; and the audience is clued into the film's overarching themes.

An example of this is the opening of the magnificent comedy *When Harry Met Sally...* As the scene begins, we meet two recent college grads who are sharing a ride together from Chicago to their new careers in New York. They are literally driving their own lives here in choices that happen to launch the plot. While they drive, they have wonderful dialogue that, married to fabulous performances, tells us who they are, who they think they are, and what they both want. The heart of their dialogue is a disagreement about the question "Can men and women ever be friends?" which is the theme of the movie dumped entertainingly right into the heart of the opening. As the sequence ends, we get some nice, loving looks at this project's arena, Manhattan, providing an appropriate start to the screenwriter's feature-length valentine to New York. It's a highly complex, masterful opening that does everything it needs to in a seamless, harmonized way.

d. Death by Visual Cliché

Visual clichés are shortcuts taken by screenwriters to try to reveal an inner life, to get through exposition more quickly, or to indicate subtext. The worst ideas are usually the first ones that pop into a writer's mind, mainly because he or she has already seen them done on the screen many, many times. Many of the following you will immediately recognize from movies you have seen. The others are things we see in bad movies and screenplays every day. If you find your script contains one of the following, find a more creative visual solution to reveal the same information.

1. The character stares into a mirror, pool of water, window, or anything shiny, just before a self pep talk, or else to figure out how he's gotten into the mess he's in.

2. A character splashes water onto his face, for clarity or as a symbol of him pulling himself together.

3. The double cliché: The character splashes water onto his face and then stares at himself in the mirror.

4. The character stares at photographs to indicate that he or she misses someone.

5. The character sits on a dock, rock, boat, or chair staring at the water or a sunset.

6. The character walks into a semi-dark church and stares at the front.

7. The character stares at... [insert anything]

8. The character is introduced by a shot of their legs getting out of a car.

9. The character is introduced lying facedown in bed and then slamming the alarm clock when it goes off. He's late.

10. The character, who is a movie director, is introduced looking through the box he is making with his thumbs and forefingers. At an angle.

11. The villain twirls his mustache, kicks a puppy, or sucks on a cigarette.

12. The roughhewn hero has a moment of sweetness with a sick child.

13. The hot chick gets introduced with a slow pan up her scantily clad bod.

14. Establishing that a character is normal or loved by panning family photographs on the wall or mantel.

15. The love-interest couple bond in a montage of them splashing in water at the beach.

16. Someone who looks dainty is handed a gun. She snaps the cartridge in and locks and loads like Rambo.

17. Someone who is having a hard time swirls and downs some adult beverage.

18. A character shakes his fist at the heavens or bangs his fist on a table or bar.

19. A character turns on the TV or radio at the exact moment he needs words of encouragement.

20. Reporters who swoop in on a scene and overwhelm a character with too many questions.

21. A character pushes the button on his answering machine, and a plot point is revealed.

22. The love-interest couple lock eyes across a room.

23. The beautiful, obnoxious person ends up falling in the mud.

24. At the restaurant, none of the characters actually eat.

25. After the wild gun battle in which many are killed, a character we care about, who has been shot, has plenty of time for poignant last words.

26. The villain ties the hero to a bomb, says a lot of nasty things, and then leaves the hero to die (which he never does because, given the time, he figures a way out).

27. The female character giving birth threatens her husband with violence.

e. Cinematic Exercises

1. What is it about your story that needs to be told on the screen, as opposed to via a novel, comic book, short story, or other medium?

2. Choose one scene from your movie and add layers to it. First and foremost, what is the beat around which it is designed? Now, add something to it to make it reveal something new about the main character. Now, add some detail of the arena. Now, find something in the scene that can hint at the theme. Can you add any more layers? Go through all of your scenes this way, adding layering.

3. Write a list of your scenes, including the first and last thing we see in each. It should look something like this:

    Scene One — (opens) Shot of a karate studio, Main Street, Little Rock, Arkansas.

    (closes) Joe facedown in the mud.

    Scene Two — (opens) Joe in his underwear, watching the clothes in the dryer.

    (closes) A female thief steals Joe's car.

    Scene Three — (opens) Joe hitchhiking, now wearing a karate uniform.

    (closes) The thief picks Joe up, not realizing it's his car she stole.

Now, create some transitions to make the scenes flow into each other more cohesively. So maybe we cut from Joe's reflection in the muddy puddle to Joe's face reflected in the spinning dryer. Another transition could be Joe in his underwear, running after his car with his hand up, cutting to Joe wearing the karate uniform, hitchhiking with his hand up.

CHAPTER 12

SECTION SUMMARY:
THE BIGGEST MISTAKES NEW SCREENWRITERS MAKE

1. **The formatting is a mess.** A screenplay is first and foremost a technical document. All the other professionals involved in the process need the script to work the way it should. Beginners tend to underestimate the importance of industry-standard formatting. It is a mistake they make at their own peril.

2. **No visual quality.** The whole screenplay is driven by dialogue. This guarantees your script will be banal, because real people rarely say what they are really thinking anyway. Dialogue should only be used as a complement to the images. Most beginning screenwriters get this backwards.

3. **The main character is not sympathetic.** Think: good, consistent, appropriate, and real. Key: We will care about a character who cares about something. It can be another person, like Mr. Incredible loves his family. It can be a vision or ideal, like Ellie's dream of going to South America in *Up*. It can also be an object, such as Ralphie's quest for an Official Red Ryder Carbine-Action Two-Hundred-Shot Range Model Air Rifle in *A Christmas Story*.

4. **No theme or purpose.** What is the story really about? What is the point? What does the main character learn from the experience? What does the audience learn from the experience?

5. **The audience doesn't know what you are going for.** They need to know right away what this story is going to be about. What are they rooting for or against?

6. **Not setting up the payoffs; not paying off the setups.** The main body of a script consists of setups that pay off. It doesn't matter which horse wins the derby if we don't have any bets on.

7. **Lack of tension. No suspense.** A good story needs a pulse and a sense of time running out. The pulse generally comes from keeping the story focused on its target. Suspense comes from the audience knowing that things are moving inexorably to a head.

8. **Not enough conflicts and storylines.** Most beginning writers focus either on the interior struggle of a character, or the external mountain that character needs to climb. Good stories need both inner and outer levels to intersect. But there need to be many more sources of conflict complicating the character's life.

9. **Bad structuring of the story.** In which a writer gives away too much too soon, and the audience gets bored because there is nothing left for them to do. Or else you don't give the audience enough clues, and you pull a resolution out of thin air. That is just annoying to the viewer.

10. **Not enough attention to transitions.** You have to give the viewer establishing shots and visual moments to let them know where they are in time and space.

11. **Subplots that distract instead of complement.** A subplot should echo or amplify the script's main theme. It isn't just a comic pause. Beginning screenwriters tend to write in subplots that never really form a seamless whole within the main theme.

12. **Mistakes in point of view.** Beware scenes featuring a point of view to which the protagonist is not privy. Say the story is about a young boy. Suddenly, you flash back to his parents' wedding. That's a POV error. The little boy could never have remembered the wedding. He wasn't born yet!

SECTION II
LINE NOTES:
SCREENPLAY STYLE AND GRAMMAR

Is this the same location or did you format that wrong?

Is this a new character? I couldn't tell.

Fix your margins. You are throwing off the project's timing.

Is that dream sequence in a flashback or in the present time?

Skip a line when the action moves outside the frame. What is this, your first script?!

CHAPTER 13

FORMATTING MATTERS

THE NOTES:

- "This is not the work of a professional."
- "Don't stretch your margins."
- "Comic Sans is not an acceptable font."
- "Stop writing CUT TO after every scene."
- "How old is this character?"
- "Where are we? I need an establishing shot!"

The Writers Guild of America estimates that 25,000 story ideas and screenplays are registered with them every year. Another 20,000 or so probably come into various Hollywood production companies and literary agencies unregistered. Perhaps only 500 or so of these projects will be optioned. Maybe a quarter of those will actually make it to the screen. Why do so many screenplays fail to make the cut? The answer begins with format problems. Based on our experience as creative executives, three quarters of the screenplays that arrive in Hollywood offices are rejected because they are improperly formatted.

75% of screenplays never get anywhere because they are improperly formatted. Say it with us: **75% of screenplays never get anywhere because they are improperly formatted.**

To development professionals, actors, directors, and agents who spend all day every day reading screenplays, an improperly formatted script screams, "I am the work of a nonprofessional." Nobody wants to work with someone who does not know the business. It's too much trouble. Dropping a script into the trash or deleting the .pdf is an easy pass to make.

Don't kid yourself. Everybody in the entertainment industry is trying to get out from under the load of paper on their desks or the endless attachments in their inboxes. Treatments, inquiries, screenplays, series bibles, résumés, and books litter every agent's and executive's desk, bookshelf, car, dining-room table, coffee table, and bedside table. They fill up their iPads and Kindles. As per the stereotype, in Hollywood you can go to any coffee shop or any restaurant at any time of day and see someone reading or working on a script. Don't give someone the chance to pass over your work with only a cursory glance because you have not taken time to make your script look like a script.

A writer once sent us a script about drug-running by the CIA in Latin America. He had pitched it over the phone, and so we asked him to send us a copy to read. When his script arrived, we opened it up, and looking at the first page, just sighed. It was a mess. Margins were wrong. Font was wrong. Spacing was wrong. And it had absolutely no sense of film grammar. Besides that, the writer (and we use the term loosely) had pasted pictures of Colombian drug lords on the insides of his covers. We read five pages just to see if maybe he had some writing talent, but ended up sending the screenplay back to him with a handout explaining screenplay format. Two days later, the man called us back, screaming over the phone, "If you really cared about social justice, then you would overlook these stupid little problems in my script!" He didn't realize that for someone who reads scripts for a living, encountering a badly formatted screenplay is like slogging through an essay by someone in a language they don't speak. It is painful, and a waste of time. A script like that is never going to go anywhere.

Nobody else is going to take the time to properly format your screenplay for you.

Trust us. Your story idea is just not that good.

Screenplay formatting is not rocket science. It is much less complicated than computer programming, but slightly more structured than prose writing. With the advent of screenwriting software programs, there is really no excuse for glaring errors in format. Final Draft is the most widely used program; and if you are planning on writing more than one screenplay in your life, it is well worth the investment. However, there are other free programs available, such as Celtx, which will do the trick if you want to dabble. Regardless of the software, you still have to know what you are doing to be able to use the computer programs correctly.

Some of these rules might seem like petty, nitpicky little annoyances designed to trip up a writer. They are. But consider that the first line of defense at a studio or agency is an unpaid intern, or an underpaid assistant whose job it is to sift through hundreds of submissions each week. Format issues are the easiest way to cull scripts into something worth the time to read — or not. No one is going to invest in a multimillion-dollar film project where an unknown writer didn't take the time to create a professional document. They just aren't.

The following rules are not an exhaustive account of every finer detail of format. There are other good books for that. Following the below guidelines, however, will keep you out of trouble.

CHAPTER 14

RULES OF SCREENPLAY STYLE

THE NOTES:

- "Casting is not the writer's job."
- "This writer is trying to be a director and an actor."
- "The language here is very clunky."
- "Take a remedial grammar course."
- "Did you proofread this?"
- "I could tell when I picked it up that it was too long."

Grammar, Spelling, and Punctuation

In this age of spellcheck and autocorrect, it is still a wonder how many projects get submitted that are stuffed with these kinds of sloppy mistakes. Nobody cares in a professional setting if you were sick in third grade on the day the lesson on "your" versus "you're" was given. People who can punctuate, spell, and draw from a wide and efficient vocabulary get hired as writers before those who cannot.

You owe it to yourself to put time into learning the rules of punctuation and the parts of speech. Screenwriters who fail to observe proper punctuation in their work run the risk of annoying their readers. Also, bad spelling and poor usage in a screenplay will surely earn your work a pass. People will figure that if you haven't done the easy thing by running spellcheck, you certainly haven't done the hard thing by creating subtext for your characters' choices.

Screenplays should be written in highly readable, engaging, and even elegant prose. As much as possible, a script should be "non-industry eyes" ready and not contain a distracting amount of technical jargon. As a rule, a screenplay should be written with complete sentences because **a screenplay is not an outline.**

Nothing But Words

A basic rule for screenwriting is not to add anything extra to your script — beyond the writing — to call attention to it. We've had people send us magazine cutouts of actors they think would be good in their movie. We've been sent sketches of set designs and costumes. We've had countless playlists for the soundtrack sent to us. All of this only distinguishes the writer as unprofessional, because none of it is the writer's job. The only thing that will sell your screenplay is actually doing your job as a writer — as measured by the quality of your script. If your screenplay is well written, the visuals will suggest themselves to the mind's-eye. Sticking a picture on your screenplay is essentially admitting that you didn't manage to create a visual image through your writing. It's a red flag for the reader.

On a practical level, even if your writing is fabulous, no development executive is going to want to walk into their boss' office with a screenplay with red flags all over it. This business is too competitive for folks to risk their own necks for you. Be smart.

Do not put a citation or theme summary on your cover, or as a header to your first page. Do not add a dedication page to your screenplay. It's very pretentious and silly at this stage of the game; it's possible that three or four other writers are going to have a crack at your script before it ends up on the screen. Save all your humble thanks for your Academy Award acceptance speech.

Binding

A script should be printed on three-hole paper and bound with brass brads: 1.5" for feature screenplays, 1.25" for teleplays. Acco is the preferred industry brand. Don't ask us why. Brads should be placed only in the top and bottom holes, because a standard-length script's pages become hard to turn if there are brads in the middle hole.

Do not waste your money on fancy bindings. We've seen scripts come spiral-bound, comb-bound, and even professionally bound. Do not do this. Back before the invention of the .pdf file, scripts would be photocopied many times over, either by an agent sending the material out to prospective buyers, or by a producer distributing the material to various departments. Fancy bindings made this difficult. While it's rare today that scripts are actually printed out, make sure you observe the two-brad rule.

Font

The industry-standard font for screenwriting is Courier Size 12. Do not — under any circumstances — use any other font or type size. We guarantee you that your work will get passed over if you do.

This rule has to do with the screen time your script represents. One page of a properly formatted screenplay in Courier Size 12 will equal roughly one minute of screen time. No one has any idea how much a page of Arial type will equal on the screen.

Screenplay Length

Historically, the preferred screenplay length has been 120 pages. In recent years, however, 120 pages has really become the maximum length at which a spec screenplay will be considered. A writer just starting out should aim for the length to be closer to 100 pages. This is all about box office. Most theaters will run five shows a day at three-hour intervals. A film that runs three hours, or 180 pages, will mean one less show a day.

Some beginners will argue that many blockbusters run close to three hours. When you are working on the level of Peter Jackson or David O. Selznick, you can do it, too, but it is better to take heed of the great master, Alfred Hitchcock, who said: "The length of a film should be directly related to the endurance of the human bladder."

Genre can also play a part in screenplay length. Family and comedy genres typically run shorter, while dramas and historical pieces run longer.

Copyright or WGA Registration

Do not write your copyright year or WGA registration number on the cover page. This is interpreted as an accusation to the reader that you fear that they might steal your work. Appearing overly defensive doesn't add to your stature in the mind of the reader. If you really, really are the nervous type, you can add an additional last page with the copyright and WGA registration number. But we wouldn't.

Script Cover Page

The screenplay title page should be white. It is permissible to use thicker, poster-stock paper on the outside cover, mainly because a script is very often used as a coaster on a reader's desk. Have the title alone on the outside cover with the standard cover sheet on regular paper immediately following.

On a standard cover page, the title of the work should be centered in the top half and be in caps. Some writers also underline the title here. The main note is to avoid fancy fonts, photos, dedications, citations, and cover designs.

Drop another four lines after the title. In caps and lower case, type: `Written by`, `Screenplay by`, `An Original Screenplay by`, or `Created by` — whichever applies to your particular script. This should also be centered on the page. Drop another two lines and beneath this, type your name in caps and lower case, centering this as well.

Drop down another four lines and write `CURRENT REVISION`; and, one line beneath it, type the date.

In the lower, right corner, type your name, address, phone number, and email, or those of your agent or manager. These should also be single-spaced, in caps and lower case.

If the script was written for a particular company or producer, their name and address should appear on the bottom, left side of the cover page.

In each corner, the top lines should be parallel to each other, and end at least one inch above the bottom of the page.

See Appendix B for a correctly formatted title page.

The Look of a Screenplay

The pages of your screenplay should look appealing enough to read. They should be a blend of dialogue and description with a lot of white space. A page full of dense prose feels too heavy, and will invariably see the reader skimming through as opposed to reading every word.

On the other hand, when we open a script and see page-long speeches everywhere, we know the script is not the work of a professional. Film is a visual medium in which visuals should be as carefully plotted out as any clever lines of dialogue.

The Screenplay's First Page

Special rules apply to a screenplay's first page:

1. At the top of your script's first page, type the title again all in caps, centered and underlined. This is the first and last time you should use underlining in your screenplay.

2. Skip two spaces and on the left-hand side, 1.5" in, type FADE IN:

3. No page number is needed on the first page of the script. After page 1, numbers should be located in the top right-hand corner, 1" from the top, 1" from the right edge, followed by a period.

See Appendix C for a correctly formatted first page.

Screenplay Margins

Every page of the screenplay needs to be configured with the following margins. These are not optional. Again, correct margins ensure that a page will equal roughly one minute of screen time.

Top and bottom margins — 1"

Left-side description margin — 1.5"

Right-side description margin — 1"

Dialogue margin — Left side — 2.5"

Right side — 2"

See Appendix D for a correctly formatted interior page.

Capitalization in Your Screenplay

These elements should always be typed in caps:

1. **Introduction of a Character** — The first time a character appears, his name should be written in caps. Any character who has more than three lines in the screenplay should be named. No actor wants to say they played "1st Man" in a screenplay.

2. **Character Name Over Dialogue** — Example:

```
                  JOHN
      You're new here, I think.
```

3. **Extras** — Casting directors will need to know what kind and how many extras to hire. Examples:

```
A cadre of TEENAGE GIRLS swoons behind the
ropes.

GRADUATES in caps and gowns proceed across
the lawn.
```

4. **Shots and Transitional Indicators** — Screenplays always begin with FADE IN and end with FADE OUT. Other shot choices can be indicated as necessary (i.e., CU for CLOSE UP; PULL BACK; DISSOLVE TO; MATCH CUT TO; MATCH DISSOLVE TO; FADE TO BLACK; ESTABLISHING; et cetera)

5. **Sluglines** — The heading of every new scene that provides the cast and crew with the location and time of day. Examples:

    ```
    EXT. NYC — WALL STREET — DAY (1865)

    INT. OFFICE BUILDING — LOBBY — DAY

    INT / EXT CAR / LIVING ROOM — DAY
    ```

6. **Sound Effects** — Use caps for any on-screen or off-screen sounds that will have to be manufactured in a lab by a sound technician. If it is a sound that an actor can make with their voice in the scene, it doesn't have to be capitalized; but otherwise, the sound designer will go through your script looking for capitalized sounds that he or she will have to create. Examples:

    ```
    Somewhere nearby, a CARRIAGE ROLLS TO A
    STOP.

    The tiger GROWLS low in his throat.

    Outside, THUNDER CRASHES and RAIN FALLS.
    ```

7. **Special Effects** — Again, for any effect that will have to be generated in a lab, the entire effect can be indicated by SFX: and then written in all caps. Examples:

    ```
    SFX: JOHN GROWS FROM SHORT TO TALL in a
    matter of seconds.

    SFX: THE WIND WHIPS THROUGH THE GRASS,
    TURNING IT INTO AN ARMY OF GREENISH MINI-
    SOLDIERS.
    ```

    As more and more CGI has become the norm for nearly every project, screenwriters have been dropping the SFX: heading and just writing the desired effect in caps. The main thing is to isolate the effect so the line producer knows how much money might be needed to create backgrounds and other images in a lab.

8. **Subject of the Shot** — This is a way to indicate a close-up without invading the director's province by actually using that language in the screenplay. Examples:

```
MARY SMITH

rubs her eyes and moans.

THE YOUNG BULLFIGHTER

pats the sweat off his forehead.
```

Line-Spacing Rules

The following should all be single-spaced: dialogue, description lines, and parenthetical character directions.

In your description lines, separate the visuals as much as possible, shot by shot, into separate paragraphs. Understanding that it is ultimately the director's call how to shoot the screenplay, the writer should still be laboring to time the project as close as possible to how it will play out on the screen. Make "1 shot = 1 paragraph" a screenwriting habit.

The following places should be double-spaced: between the speeches of different characters; between the narrative description and a character's name; before and after sluglines; and before and after any camera or transitional directions.

Rules for Writing Dialogue

Dialogue margins should be strictly followed. They are shorter than description lines because it is understood that actors will need to add time to the playing of the line for dramatic purposes. Once again, the length of the dialogue line has everything to do with preserving the "one page equals one minute of screen time" equation of a professional screenplay.

Dialogue lines should not exceed 3.5" long. Dialogue margins start 2.5" from the left-hand side of the page and end 2" from the right-hand side of the page.

In a screenplay, the images are always described before the lines of dialogue that are being spoken over them. This is because light moves faster than sound, and we see things before we hear them.

Continued Dialogue

Never separate a character's name from the dialogue line that follows it. Avoid splitting a character's speech from one page to the next. It can't always be helped, but it's always distracting when it happens, and a mess for actors who are highlighting their lines as a whole. When it's absolutely necessary to split a speech, observe this format method:

In the parenthetical margin, type (MORE) at the bottom of the speech on the first page so that the reader knows that there will be "more" dialogue connected to that speech on the following page. On the next page, after the character's name write (CONT'D) beside the character's name in the dialogue. Here's an example:

```
                VINNIE
    It's always about them, Austin.
          (MORE)
```

2.

```
                VINNIE (CONT'D)
    Never about you. And now it's
    over.
```

If a character's dialogue is interrupted by a description line, write (CONT'D) after typing the character's name again. For example:

```
                SUE
    Emily? Emily, I know you are
    here somewhere.

    Sue looks around the stable. She catches
    sight of some movement in the corner.

                SUE (CONT'D)
    Ah, ha! There you are!
```

Voiceover Versus Off Screen Versus Off Camera

In dialogue, the convention is that whichever character has the line is the subject of the shot. When this is not the case, there are three indicators to represent a different way that dialogue is to be delivered.

> **VOICEOVER** *(V.O.): This is used for non-diegetic dialogue, which means speech that cannot be heard by the characters on the screen. This is the way narration is indicated.*
>
> **OFF SCREEN** *(O.S.): This means that a character is speaking from a place beyond the current set and is not visible on the screen. He or she is down the hall or in the next room or on the phone or on the radio or out there in the yard heard through the window.*
>
> **OFF CAMERA** *(O.C.): This is to be used when a character is speaking in the location of the scene, but is not being shown on camera. This would be used if we wanted to watch one character's face while another character is speaking. It could be used as a speech by one character to cover a tracking shot taking in members of the audience.*

Using Parenthetical Directions

These are brief instructions to the actors that should generally indicate actions that reveal character psychology where it isn't already obvious from context. Don't use parentheticals unless they provide information not covered or clear in the dialogue or progress of the scene. In other words, let the actors act. Let the director direct. Don't just use parentheticals as fillers or timing mechanisms if an actor would be liable to do it anyway.

Don't write a parenthetical where the emotion is clear from the dialogue:

```
                    MARK
              (angry)
     I hate you, you idiot!
```

Do use a parenthetical when a character is speaking facetiously or contrary to how they are feeling:

```
                   BUTCH
              (strokes her cheek)
      You're really horrid, you know?
```

Also, avoid using adverbs as parentheticals. Don't say "nervously" or "angrily" or "wearily." Give the actors something to do which instead reveals their inner state. Example:

```
                    EMILY
        They say that time heals wounds.
                (slams the window)
        Time never heals anything.
```

Do not capitalize the first letter of the first word in a parenthetical notation.

Any time a parenthetical is going to be as long a line as the dialogue, it should be written as straight description minus the parentheses. Again, parentheticals should never be extended through two lines. If you have to move to another line, write the parenthetical as a description line and then continue the dialogue as shown above.

Rules for Sluglines

INT. and EXT. must be written at the start of every new scene (the slugline) to indicate location. INT. indicates "interior" and EXT. indicates "exterior"; each should be followed by a M-dash and the time of day. A slugline is primarily meant to indicate the location for the scene, and whether it needs to be day or night. Avoid saying things like *twilight, dawn, evening,* or *early afternoon,* as these really have no meaning in an actual shoot.

Examples:

```
INT. CLASSROOM — DAY

EXT. DRUG STORE — SIDE ENTRANCE — NIGHT
```

Never separate your slugline from the action line that follows it. One reason you should buy screenplay software is that it automatically does this for you as you add things to your script and the lines get pushed across pages.

Sluglines should be standardized so that all of the scenes being shot in the same location can be identified and printed out together.

Use the same language in the slugline as you did originally when you return to a location. Your production designer will go through your script and count how many different locations he or she needs to create. If you use three different names for the same location, he will count those as three different sets. In other words, don't call a location JOHN'S HOUSE in one slugline, THE HOUSE in another, and McCAFFREY'S HOUSE in another. Most screenplay software programs keep track of or list the locations you have created, and will prompt you to use one when you start a new scene. But, to maintain consistency, the writer still needs to be thinking of this issue before writing a slugline.

Sluglines should always move from the general, larger world to the more specific. There should be a space before and after each M-dash.

Examples:

```
INT. NEW YORK CITY — PLAZA HOTEL — BAR —
NIGHT

EXT. THE RUSSIAN STEPPE — A VILLAGE — DAY
```

If the entire movie takes place in one city, such as New York, then it is only necessary to mention the city in the establishing-shot slugline at the beginning of the piece.

INT./EXT. *Slashes are a variation on the slugline that are used when action is happening through a window or in two locations simultaneously. Example:*

```
INT./EXT. KITCHEN / FRONT LAWN — DAY

Mary watches the helicopter land on her
front lawn.
```

ESTABLISHING SHOT: *An establishing shot is a very wide shot that allows the viewer to broadly contextualize the action. Establishing shots generally take in locations such as the city panorama, or a mountain range, or the Las Vegas strip. Writers generally need them in transitional moments in a screenplay when characters are changing locations.*

For example, if the action moves from Miami to New York, you probably want an establishing shot of the Big Apple before you go to any interiors. These should be indicated thusly:

```
EXT. AMHERST COUNTRYSIDE — DAY (ESTABLISHING)

INT. BIG CITY LIBRARY — THE STACKS — DAY
(ESTABLISHING)
```

Description or Action Lines

FIRST LINE UNDER A SLUGLINE: *The first line of a new scene should always be description, never dialogue. Your description line should give information about which characters and what essential props are present. It is equally important for the description line to give a sense of the tone and a feel of the place. This needs to be done elegantly and economically. The idea is to note a few key details so that the location scout and production designer know how to decorate the whole rest of the set.*

Some examples:

```
EXT. A NEW ENGLAND CEMETERY — 1895 — DAY

Fallen leaves spot the brownish, green
carpet of grass.

Here and there, bunches of flowers lean
against weathered gray stones. A BRANCH
SNAPS under a woman's foot.

INT. THE CARNEGIE HOMESTEAD — THE DINING
ROOM — NIGHT

The well-appointed table is set for a feast
for twenty. A MAID bustles into the room and
lights the centerpiece candles.
```

NO REPETITION: *Do not repeat the description-line information you already wrote in your slugline. That is, do not do this:*

```
INT. BARN — DAY

John is in the barn.
```

We know that. You already told us that we were in the barn in the slugline. You should be telling us what John is doing.

AVOID ADVERBS: Avoid using adverbs in action lines. Give your actors something to do that will be a visual representation of their inner life. For example, don't say:

```
John nervously sits at his desk.
```

Say instead:

```
John taps a pencil on his desktop. When the
alarm clock in front of him goes off, the
pencil breaks in his fingers.
```

AVOID GERUNDS: Avoid using gerunds in action lines. Gerunds break up the power of your prose and also take up too much space. For example, don't say:

```
Mary is sitting on a bench in the corner
licking an ice-cream cone.
```

Write instead:

```
Mary sits on a bench and licks an ice-cream
cone.
```

AVOID ORPHANS: Particularly in description and action lines, avoid leaving one word alone on a line — these are termed "orphans." The technical reason for this is, again, it throws off the timing of the whole piece. The aesthetic reason is that the one lonely word there makes the script look choppy. The artistic and stylistic reason is that with only a hundred or so pages in which to tell a story, a writer needs to be jealous of all the real estate she or she cedes by leaving lines so underutilized. If there is just one orphan on every page, at the end of the movie there will be nearly two pages that could have been much better spent in telling the story.

Camera and Technical Directions

Be very sparing when using camera directions. People in the business are very wary of writers who are trying to be directors or cinematographers. A good writer rarely needs to mention camera shots. If the writing is visual enough, it will be clear to the reader what is appearing on the screen.

Don't use any expressions like "*We see* John walk in," or "*The camera follows* John at the counter," or "John *appears in the shot.*"

Especially "*we see.*" Get rid of these. We know we're seeing it if you are describing it in your screenplay!

Putting a character's name or an object in caps alone on a line tells us it is a close-up. You don't need to also use the signifier CU.

TRACKING SHOT: *This is a long shot that moves around a location taking in details. The visuals revealed in the tracking shots should be listed and then followed by "…"*

Example:

```
A church revival is in full swing.

The CHOIR LEADER beats the air to the tune
of a hymn...

A YOUNG BOY and GIRL in the choir flirt with
each other...

A CROWD of believers wave their hands in the
air and weep...
```

INSERT: *This is a close-up shot that will generally be filmed without the actors. It is used to show some detail that will be a cutaway in the scene.*

Example: You are describing a battle scene during the Mexican-American War, and you want to show a map of the territory over which the fighting is taking place. Write:

```
INSERT — MAP
of Russia, 1834
```

INSERT *is also used when we need to see something a character is reading, or the time on her watch. These shots are done separately and then inserted into a scene during editing.*

SUPER: *Is the abbreviation for "superimpose," and refers to a title or other image being added in editing over the images on the screen. The typical usage is:*

```
A lovely town green with the fall colors
bursting from every tree.
SUPER: AMHERST, MA, 1840
```

An example of another use of superimposition is in the opening of the film Apocalypse Now *in which the image of the main character's upside-down head gets placed atop images of the forest, a fiery battle, and helicopters. The point of the superimposition here is to show that the images are in the character's mind.*

INTERCUT: *The interfacing of two scenes meant to be one scene. It can be used effectively to show what is happening simultaneously between two subjects.*

Example: A scene of a man and a woman making their wedding vows could ironically be intercut with the two characters having affairs or flirting with other people.

Transitional Instructions

In a feature screenplay, transitional instructions such as DISSOLVE, FADE IN, MATCH CUT, MATCH DISSOLVE, or CUT TO are editing techniques and should be used sparingly. Leave those decisions to the editor and director.

Having said that, occasionally a writer can indicate a powerful transition that will impact the theme or indicate the elapse of time in the story.

MATCH CUT: *A matching of the subject of a shot in one scene with a similar subject or related subject in the next scene.*

Example: A book cover showing a picture of Abraham Lincoln matched to a scene with the actual president Lincoln.

```
INSERT BOOK COVER: A faded Brady photograph
of the Gettysburg Address.

                          MATCH CUT TO:

EXT. GETTYSBURG — DAY (1863)
The rain-soaked crowd stands hushed and
numb. Lincoln looks up from the podium.
```

Match-cutting can also be used to convey a deeper meaning or connection between two objects.

Example: Matching a baby bird crying for food in one scene to a human baby sucking a bottle makes a statement about the nature of babies. Matching a painter whitewashing a building to a woman putting on makeup indicates an attitude about the purpose of makeup.

DISSOLVE: *Is often used to indicate a time lapse, flashback, or* *dream sequence. It should not be confused with cutting from shot to shot. A dissolve is a blending of two shots achieved by the simultaneous fading out of one image (the screen darkens) and the fading in of another image, in reverse density, from dark to medium. The first picture disappears into the next picture. It involves the merging of two pictures, and never the use of a blank screen or a dark screen.*

Montage Versus Series of Shots

MONTAGE: *The factor distinguishing a montage from a series of shots is that in a montage, the order or sequence of the shots is critical to the narrative. The juxtaposition of images holds within it a deeper meaning. Note that all of the locations need to have already been established and described.*

```
MONTAGE — MICHAEL BECOMES THE GODFATHER

1. Michael holds the baby while a priest
recites prayers.

2. On a city street, AL NERI checks his
weapon.

3. The priest baptizes the baby. Michael
lights a candle.

4. Neri storms through a door and shoots
Moe Greene.
```

SERIES OF SHOTS: *Think of a series of shots as fleshing out an establishing shot. If an establishing shot gives us the broadest possible picture of an arena, a series of shots can take us inside that arena and give us a closer look around.*

Again, the order of the shots doesn't really matter.

Example:

```
SERIES OF SHOTS — A CIRCUS FINALE

» Some clowns bounce on a trampoline.

» An acrobat walks on a high wire.

» Two children eat pink cotton candy and
watch the action, riveted.
```

> » Some horses prance around in the center ring.

> » A ringmaster directs a small band.

Variations for Television Formats

Although the general rules of basic feature formatting apply, every TV show has its own special way of formatting their scripts. Try and obtain sample scripts of the show for which you are writing a spec. There are a number of resources online, as well as the WGA library, to obtain scripts. In the event that no sample script is available, or that you are writing your own pilot, here are some general rules:

> ***Act Breaks:*** *The acts are necessitated by breaks for commercials (and require considerable structural alterations in the development of a plot). Each new act begins at the top of a page. Type* ACES ONE — *double-space down, then type* FADE IN:
>
> *Your first page of Act One should have* ACT ONE *centered at the top of the first page.* END OF ACT ONE *should be centered at the bottom of the last page of the act. There is a page break at the end of each act, and each act begins halfway down a new page.*
>
> *The first page of Act Two should have* ACT TWO *centered at the top of its first page. Center* THE END *at the bottom of the last page.*

SINGLE-CAMERA FORMAT	
30-minute sitcom	28–31 pages — Two acts, approximately 13 pages each
60-minute drama	50–80 pages — Four acts, approximately 14 pages each, plus a teaser (4–6 pages) and sometimes a tag (2–4 pages)
MULTI-CAMERA FORMAT (3-Camera Technique)	
Dialogue for teleplays is double-spaced throughout, which makes the complete script for a standard hour-long series 52–59 pages long.	

CHAPTER 15

SOME ADDITIONAL FORMATTING DO'S AND DON'TS

What follows is a list of screenwriting and formatting guidelines that fall between and beyond some of the rules and definitions that govern formatting at its most basic levels.

Articles: *Don't eliminate articles (a, an, the, et cetera). A screenplay is not an outline.*

Bold: *It is better to not use boldface beyond the title. Since nobody in the business has defined exactly what bolding means in this context, you run the risk of confusing them. In treatments, bolding can be used to highlight a character's name the first time it appears; but beyond that, its use can become problematic.*

Capitals Overused: *The more you use caps, the less significance they have. They are imperative for sound effects, camera directions (like the close-up shortcut), transitional directions, and character names the first time they appear and whenever they are used over a dialogue line. Otherwise, they are distracting and confusing.*

Character Descriptions: *Don't focus your character descriptions on the one thing you'll have the least control over: the physical type of your characters. You don't want to eliminate someone from casting just because you wrote that they need to be black or very tall or blue-eyed. You can give a modicum of attention to this, but what is more important is the psychological profile of your character. You are allowed one sentence when you introduce a character* *to give us a sense of his or her attitude. Other than that, everything about them needs to be conveyed visually — the style of their dress (as opposed to specific items of clothing), the way they walk, what they notice, how other people treat them. Develop concise, evocative language for describing what a character is like on the inside.*

Close-Up Shortcut: *The close-up shortcut is a technique of creating a new camera angle without the use of a technical term, such as* CLOSE-UP, ANGLE-ON, *or* MEDIUM SHOT. *This is accomplished simply by placing the name of the subject of the shot in a paragraph all by itself in capitals.*

Here are two examples:

```
AUSTIN DICKINSON
chews on a piece of straw. He is only half listening to
his foreman talk about the farm. Suddenly, he whirls away
and throws the straw to the ground.
```

Within ongoing active description:

```
Sue drops her eyes to the church pew beside her. Austin's
SPANKING NEW GENTLEMAN'S GLOVES make a strange contrast to
HER OWN POOR, MENDED GLOVES beside them.
Sue looks back up at Austin with a coquettish smile.
```

There are a few important rules that govern the use of the "close-up shortcut."

Internal Location: *An abbreviated slugline (see "Rules for Sluglines" in Chapter 14) is only appropriate for those locations that are enclosed within a much larger location (either within an interior or an exterior). For example, when setting a scene in a nightclub, after using the general slugline:*

```
INT. NIGHTCLUB — NIGHT
```

Describe the action within the club overall, and then move the action to a specific area of the club. For instance:

```
THE BAR
TWO GUYS in trench coats occupy the last two stools at
the end of the bar, huddling over martinis.
```

Phone-Conversation Intercutting: *The simplest method of executing a phone conversation intercut between two locales is to describe both locales at* *either end of the conversation, state that you want to intercut from one scene to the next, and then just write out the dialogue until you reach the end of the conversation, choosing which locale is the last you'll see.*

It can be to your advantage to specify who is on camera and when, perhaps by changing locations whenever it is dramatically appropriate to focus on one specific character.

Props: *Do not capitalize props.*

Separating Character from Dialogue: *Never separate a character's name from the dialogue that follows it.*

Separating a Slugline from the Action Line That Follows: *Never separate your slugline from the action line that follows it. You have to figure out a way of avoiding this at the bottom of a page.*

Separating Sound from an Accompanying Visual: *Don't separate a sound effect from the visual it accompanies. It will throw off the timing of the script because in actuality, these two elements can be delivered simultaneously.*

CHAPTER 16

SECTION SUMMARY:
FORMATTING RED FLAGS THAT WILL STOP YOUR SCREENPLAY

1. **Anything attached to the script** beyond maybe a short synopsis. There should be no artwork, pictures, letters of support, location shots, proposed casting lists, newspaper clippings, or anything but the text of your screenplay.

2. **The wrong font or type size.** Courier 12 is the only professional font.

3. **Colored paper, colored fonts, fancy covers.** All of this is the mark of a nonprofessional who is trying to inappropriately garner attention.

4. **Too many pages.** People who read scripts all day can tell just by the feel of your script if it is overlong. Readers tend to reach for the shorter scripts in their pile.

5. **Grammar errors, spelling mistakes, and typos.** People will figure that if you haven't bothered to take care of the easy things, you certainly won't have addressed the much harder matters of plot, character, and layering. A producer told us once that if she finds three mistakes on a page, she dumps the whole script in the trash.

6. **Overwriting.** The page should not look heavy with long paragraphs of prose. Besides being a slog to read, a script that looks like this indicates a writer who is a control freak. Don't over-choreograph action sequences and fight scenes. Just make the

script shorter so that the director has extra time with which to experiment.

7. **Underwriting.** A screenplay is not an outline.

8. **Doing other people's jobs.** Don't try to cast the movie by describing the characters in precise physical terms. Don't stipulate details of place and character and props unless they are absolutely needed for the tone and story.

9. **Don't overuse camera directions.** A screenplay should be able to be read by people who haven't mastered formatting terms and industry lingo. Also, the concern of the screenwriter is what happens on the screen. It is the director's job to figure out the logistics of shooting this material.

10. **Using parentheticals to direct actors.** Parentheticals should only be used when the emotions in play are not obvious from the context. It's the actor's job to figure out the five best ways to say the line.

11. **Nonexistent transitions.** Writers need to include all the little location-establishing shots so that the audience doesn't get lost. The editor might eliminate some of these in the final cut, but at least the director will have sent the shots into postproduction.

SECTION III
THE WORKING SCREENWRITER

CHAPTER 17

SO NOW WHAT?

THE NOTES:

- **"The script reads like a first draft."**
- **"The script was rife with errors."**
- **"It's a few passes away."**
- **"The writer needs professional feedback."**

You've typed FADE OUT. You have an actual "whole enchilada" first draft of your screenplay. Hurray! Now what do you do? Time to send it to Spielberg?

No.

As Churchill said after the Battle of Britain, "This is not the end. It is not even the beginning of the end. But it may be the end of the beginning." You have much more to do before your script is ready to send to any industry professional, or even just a paid script consultant.

After writing FADE OUT:

1. Celebrate
2. Refresh and Step Back
3. Reread and Revise
4. Get Feedback from Peers
5. Get Feedback from Professionals
6. Revise Again
7. Call It Done
8. Get It Out There
9. Start Your Next Project

You may be tempted, but do not skip any of these steps!

Celebrate

No, really. Every draft is a major accomplishment. Did you know that most people who start a screenplay never finish even one draft? Take a moment to relish the fact that your first draft means that you have achieved a major milestone. Soak in that accomplishment. If you want to be a working, professional writer, it matters that you celebrate your milestones, and not just the ones attached to a check. You will have a much happier existence if you see your primary victory as successfully completing the work you have set yourself to do. Go buy yourself one of those ball-caps that says WRITER.

Refresh and Step Back

Next, give yourself some time off. Ideally, take at least a week off from looking at your draft and go do something else. Anything else. If you are under deadline and can't afford that amount of time, at the very least, take twenty-four hours to get physically and mentally away from your script. The time off will offer an invaluable opportunity for you to see your work in a new way, which will in turn help your writing much more profoundly than any amount of time staring at the screen would.

Reread and Revise

Once you are refreshed, it's time to reread what you've written. Do not skip to revisions before you've read your script the whole way through! It amazes us how many clients come wanting feedback on work they've never actually fully read themselves. If *they* won't even read it, what makes them think others will want to?

We recommend printing out a draft as opposed to reading it all on a computer. Holding actual pages in your hand reinforces the fact that your script is *real*, and this physical proof can have many positive benefits upon the writer's psyche. Yes, we realize this suggestion is not "green," but we believe the psychological benefits outweigh the environmental risks. We writers deal in the imaginary so much that sometimes the physical evidence of our work is necessary to convince us that we've accomplished something. Another reason to print out a script at this stage is for copyright purposes. It's a good idea to hold onto an early draft of your work in both digital and printed form. If you're a stickler for not printing pages (or you ran out of ink), then at the very least, save the draft as a .pdf and read it like an eBook on the tablet of your choosing.

Take a couple of hours without any distractions to read your draft the whole way through, resisting the urge to stop and tweak anything. Just inhale the whole thing in one sitting, as if you were sitting in the theater watching it unfold on the screen. When you finish, stretch and take a break before jotting down any notes. When it's time for notes, filter your thoughts through an objective lens, and first consider the meta-questions: At what places in the story am I engaged? At what places am I not engaged? Which characters pop off the pages? Which feel more like props? What are the key emotional moments of the piece? What's clear and what's unclear?

We'll go into a more extensive checklist in the Rewriting chapter; but for now, keep your notes simple and broad. Bearing them in mind, you can then go back through your script and mark all the little glaring things you saw during your read-through (while resisting the temptation to stop and fix them immediately).

Okay. You've read for clarity. The typos are fixed. *Now* is my screenplay ready to send out?

No.

Now your screenplay is ready for the next round of revisions. Your goal with this round is to do everything you know how to do to make it better. Try not to get too hung up on the areas you don't know how to fix. Focus instead on the areas that you feel most confident revising. If you find yourself getting stuck on a particular area, just move to the next thing. Read our chapter on rewriting, and make the most you can of it. Read our section on format and make sure you've edited your material to the best of your ability. This step might take days, weeks, or even months. Your mantra for this step is, "Do the best you can." There is a sweet spot between laziness and perfectionism for which you are aiming. Expect that your screenplay won't be perfect yet, but resolve the things that are in your power to resolve.

Now can I send it out?

Yes!... but not to producers, agents, or even your mom. You are now at a stage where you need feedback on your script. However, it must be the right kind of feedback, because your script is at a fragile stage. People who are untrained in the screenwriting process should not read your script yet, nor should anyone that you need to impress. You need feedback from two kinds of people — peers who are trained in the craft, and professional mentors and script consultants.

Get Feedback from Peers

If you are in a writers' group, this is the stage where you need to have your group read and give notes. If you are not in a group, or live in an area where you are the only screenwriter in a thousand-mile radius, you can still benefit from peer feedback. There are many resources for you in the digital age to connect with other writers. Find online groups and join discussion boards. Figure out the main areas you are stuck on and ask for specific feedback on those areas. Review our chapters on giving and receiving notes when you process feedback from your peers.

Get Feedback from Professionals

This is also a good time to invest in quality feedback from a professional script consultant. Don't settle for cheap, gimmicky "coverage" notes. They won't help you at this stage. What you need are specifics on story, character, structure, theme, dialogue, format, and marketplace factors. The kind of notes you need require a minimum of one full day's work from the consultant. You should also invest in a phone consultation where you can ask questions in addition to receiving written feedback. Make sure you are getting your money's worth by being prepared for this step! Submitting a script too soon and not considering the areas where you have questions is a waste of resources for you, and it annoys the consultant. Your professionalism matters now as much as it does in future stages.

Revise Again

Once you've gathered and processed your feedback, it's time to go back to the computer for the next revision stage. Depending on the kind of feedback you received, this can either be a long or a short process. Nevertheless, it is an extremely important one. Up until now, your baby has been almost entirely formed by the machinations in your own head. You are now incorporating feedback based on how the story is perceived by others. Some writers are better than others at stepping outside themselves and seeing other points of view. How you fare incorporating outside notes will make or break your project from this point forward. Writing from here onward will become a highly collaborative process. Proceed with caution.

Call It Done

You've incorporated. You've revised. You've even sent it out again for notes, and this time it came back with rave reviews.

NOW can I send it out?

Not quite yet. There's one more tiny, but very important, step: Call it done.

By "done," we mean that the script is ready to send out into the world. This, by industry standards, is now officially your first draft. If it gets optioned or sold, you'll likely have another long road of revisions. We'll get to that. However, it is important to your writer soul to call it "done." That means you've stopped revising it. That means there is nothing else you'd fix or change (for now). Having a script that's "done" is cause for major celebration. So do that. And then...

Get It Out There

Yes, young Padawan, it is finally time. Paper (or .pdf) the town, if you'd like. We recommend having a strategy for this step, which we'll cover in the next few chapters. Don't be shy. After all, it's done. It's time to get it in front of people.

Start Your Next Project

The truth is, you are never done with a movie project until you are sitting in the theater watching the credits roll. Moving on to the next project in the action of a professional writer who is not putting all their eggs into one script-basket. Also, after starting on the next project, you will be amazed how much perspective you will find on your previous one. Moving on diminishes so much of the urgency that we writers can attach to a project. We need to see each project not as the Holy Grail, but as just another story upon which we will work as our careers unfold.

CHAPTER 18

REWRITING

THE NOTES:

- "Did the writer even read his own script before he sent it to me?"
- "This script is choppy. It doesn't flow."
- "So many sloppy errors."
- "This script is so not reader-friendly."
- "There's a good idea here, but the writer needs to make two or three more passes before it's ready."

I hate writing. I love having written.
— DOROTHY PARKER

There are a couple of camps into which we writers tend to fall. One is the prolific first-draft camp. These are writers who have many scripts, all of which are first drafts. While the number of pages they have under their belts might be impressive, their career stagnates because they are unable to go deeper with their writing. They tend to cling to their first drafts, unwilling to dismantle them for the sake of making them stronger. These writers tend to appear accomplished, but then lose out when they can't execute notes or make changes in a collaborative setting. They need to learn to rely on others for feedback, and to continuously challenge themselves to go deeper.

The other one is the "My preciousss!" camp. These are the people who maybe only have one script, but they've rewritten it fifty million times. Like Gollum, they cannot let go. They tweak and tweak, never calling it done, fearing that someone will reject their work before they've had a chance to tweak just one more thing. These writers often feel unaccomplished because they have very little finished product to show for all their hard work; in turn, they give up on themselves too soon. The truth is, these writers just need more time (and confidence) to develop their skills. These writers tend to be thinking deeply about their work, and if they persevere will not only find their way but will create great works of art. That is, if you can pry it out of their hands.

There is a phenomenon that our friend, veteran TV writer Ron Austin, calls the "one-and-a-half-script hump." That is, by the time a writer has gotten through one and a half scripts, suddenly they realize that writing is *hard*. Inspiration and optimism often motivate the writing of first scripts; but along the way, reality sets in. A second script is started with the determination that it will be better than the first. But *how*? Writing requires discipline, which is hard — earned through many tedious days of learning and practice. If a writer can persevere and complete a second script, their chances for success are good.

No one would expect to sit down at a piano and play Chopin on the first try, yet so many people approach screenwriting with this notion.

Having something to say and knowing how to say it are vastly different things. Often, writers will be able to identify what's wrong with their script long before they are able to execute the changes to fix it. It can be a paralyzing experience, but also an important one to work through. The only way to master the craft of writing is to keep writing. A lot.

There are some things that become easier over time. When we were first starting out, it would take us five or six drafts to be able to accomplish what we can now do in one draft. However, that doesn't mean that the process of writing is any *easier*, or that we write *less*. It simply means that we are able to go farther and deeper into the craft than we used to.

Rewriting comes in many forms. Many writers will self-edit and rewrite as they craft their first drafts. Some writers prefer to be totally free from their inner editors as they spit out a first draft. Whatever your process is, inevitably, more revisions lie ahead.

There are many layers contributing to the final incarnation of a polished draft. We recommend rereading your script with your focus on each of these areas:

1. Clarity
2. Tone and Pace
3. Plot
4. Character
5. Theme
6. Dialogue
7. Music and Sound
8. Visual Imagery
9. Spectacle
10. Format, Spelling, Punctuation, and Grammar

Clarity

Clarity is king. The first questions for any first draft are: "Is it clear?" "Does it say what I want it to say?" "Does it make sense?" If you want, have someone read your draft and give you feedback simply regarding whether your piece is understandable as a story. It might sound like a simple fix, but clarity is often overlooked when working with a draft. It won't matter how clever your characters are, or how brilliant your theme is, if your story is unclear.

Tone and Pace

Like clarity, tone is often overlooked, especially in a first draft. Read through the whole draft of your script looking for the emotional highs and lows of your piece. Does the tone match the genre? If it's a comedy, does it make you laugh? If it's a drama, does it make you cry? Note the areas where it feels flat, or where the tone might need to change.

Does your story read quickly, or is it a thick slog to get through? Does your story seem too long or too short? Are things happening too quickly or too slowly? Depending on the tone of your piece, is there an appropriate amount of action and rest? If necessary, get some preliminary feedback specifically on pacing. The note you want to hear is that your script is a "fast read." That means your pacing is keeping the reader interested.

Plot

Next, read and revise for plot. Is there a beginning, middle, and end? Go through our section on plot. Are each of the necessary parts of the beginning present and accounted for? Is there enough conflict driving the plot through the middle? Does the story resolve satisfactorily? Do the beats and scenes build upon one another?

Character

Look for your character's wants and needs. Are they evident in the story? Is your main character making active, visual choices that drive the story forward? Does your main character grow and change? Does your main character make a sacrifice or face his own fears? How about the supporting characters?

Chances are, when writing your first draft, you were looking at the story through the point of view of your main character. Read through it again from the perspective of each of the supporting characters, and see what insights you find. It's a good idea to create a character report that shows the number of lines and scenes for each character. Final Draft has a feature that does this simply. The scene count alone can often be very revealing: Do the supporting characters have enough to do in your story? Do some characters need to be cut or combined?

Theme

We believe that stories need at least a working theme, or a general concept of what a story is really about in order to begin, so now is the time to define and hone that theme. Many first drafts carry the beginnings of multiple themes. Make a list of the ones you see emerging (or ask someone to help you identify them).

Of these, which is the primary one upon which you want your story to center? Comb through every scene to bring that theme forward, and cut back on the others. Yes, you may need to cut back on other cool stuff that doesn't serve your theme. Trust us: it's worth it.

Dialogue

The best way to see if your dialogue is working is to have actors read your script aloud. Most first-draft dialogue needs to be trimmed or have more subtext worked into it.

Music and Sound

What does this story sound like? Is there anything to enhance in this scene that could heighten your tone?

Visual Imagery

Visually, what can you add to this story to give it dimension and depth? How can the production design contribute to the theme, tone, and spectacle of this story?

Spectacle

Ascertain the key cinematic moments of your story. First of all, do you have any? Secondly, where? Often, action sequences or scenes requiring special effects need special attention and framing to properly translate a writer's vision to the screen.

Format, Spelling, Punctuation, and Grammar

After all of the revisions have been made to the content of the story, read your script through in search of formatting errors. Make sure your locations are consistent. Are you using active verbs in your action lines? Look up formatting rules for areas such as intercuts or montages that you haven't committed to memory yet.

Last, but certainly not least, read through one more time for edits. Spellcheck. Read it again, looking for improper word usage that spellcheck didn't catch. If this is not an area of strength for you, find someone to read and edit your script. Don't skip this step!

CHAPTER 19

STORY CURRENCY:

LOGLINES, SYNOPSES, PROPOSALS, BEAT SHEETS, AND TREATMENTS

THE NOTES:

- "I asked for a logline and he gave me Lincoln's Second Inaugural."
- "The investor just wants the story without all the technical jargon."
- "That's not a logline; it's a greeting card."
- "This synopsis is too pitchy. I just need the story."
- "Overwritten treatment. The movie will run short."

People often note that story is the currency of Hollywood. In the same way that the gold in Fort Knox is the real value represented by our dollars and cents, story is the value that underlies all the equipment, professionals, studios, and sub-industries that make up the entertainment business.

Just like different denominations of currency represent more or less gold, the entertainment business has evolved a whole series of written documents that represent different points on the spectrum of story value. In this metaphor, a screenplay is the $100 bill, because it represents the most complete expression of a story idea in writing.

A confusion prevalent in the industry stems from the many different names given to the same basic, few story products. In the same way people call a dollar a buck, a greenback, a clam, or a one-spot, Hollywood can call the same two sheets of paper a summary, a synopsis, a short synopsis, a one-page, a leave-behind, or a short treatment.

All these different names are not helpful to a writer trying to deliver what a producer wants. So, for clarity purposes here, we are going to put official names on the basic story-development tools, and add a new one of our own making. But know that in every job, the writer needs to clarify with the producer, "So, when you say you want a treatment, you mean... ?"

a. A Penny of Your Thoughts: Loglines

A logline is the pitchy answer to the question writers are asked eight hundred times a year: "So, what are you working on?" It is the hook that gets busy agents and producers to take a look at your script. So you have to be ready with lovely loglines for your projects at any moment, just in case.

Loglines originated in old Hollywood, in the dusty vaults of the major studios. Unproduced screenplays were stored in tall piles on warehouse shelves. With scripts stacked maybe fifteen to twenty high, a mess occurred whenever hungry directors came through looking for their next project. So studio archivists began writing a sentence on the spine of each script which detailed the basics of the story. The description needed to indicate the genre, the main action, and the scope of the piece.

Over the years, the logline has evolved into the basic unit of a story concept. Most of them aren't even worth a penny, because, as everyone always says, "You can't sell an idea." Still, once an idea is fleshed out, the logline is irreplaceable as the first pitch that either gets you an appreciative nod and a business card, or a glazed-over look.

For a writer at the beginning of the creative process, it can be helpful to condense a story into a logline to see if it has "Cineplex potential." Imagine a wife standing in line outside a box office. What few words can she say about a movie to get her husband into the theater? A logline gets to the heart of what the movie will be, and how the experience of it will feel. It zones in on the "high concept" of a piece.

Just as in those old studio days, the virtue of a good logline is that it conveys the *genre*, *tone*, *time period*, and *basic action* of the story. Also helpful is if the logline suggests the theme and the main struggle of the main character. Some examples include:

Gone With the Wind: Echoing the tragedy of the Civil War in the antebellum South, high-spirited Scarlett O'Hara loses everything, but survives to discover her true identity.

Titanic: While the great ship is lost, Rose is saved in every way that a person can be saved.

The Incredibles: In a time when superheroes are illegal, the greatest of them all must find a way to save his family of superheroes from a new nemesis and then live out his destiny.

When we ask newbie writers for loglines, sometimes we get "taglines" in response. Taglines are the shticky one-liners that you see on movie posters like "Better Late Than Never..." (*The 40-Year-Old Virgin*) or "Jack Frost Is More Than a Myth" (*Rise of the Guardians*). Writers should never burden themselves with movie-poster slogans. Instead, focus on conveying the plot, theme, and tone of your story in a succinct way.

It should be noted that loglines are very much a creature of the studio system, which in recent years has tended to produce movies that are so formulaic as to be well-suited to one-sentence summarization. (Many projects from the last two decades are so similar that they could probably just be assigned a category number from one to ten, as in: #1. This is *Speed* in a shopping mall / on a train / on a plane. #2. Action hero with funny sidekick saves the world. #3. Twentysomethings in Manhattan / L.A. are bad at love. #4. Bad guy with a heart gets in over his head. #5. Corporate guy discovers the importance of family...) So note that loglines almost never serve quirky stories well. Quirky stories are the stuff of the burgeoning independent-cinema world in which being able to "sum it up in a sentence" is regarded with distaste.

Logline Exercise: One logline formula to try out and evolve in your own way is: "It's a [genre] about [character] who does [action] to get [object], but learns [lesson]." Once you have the hang of the basic structure, feel free to put your own spin on it.

b. Putting Your Two Cents In: A Story Synopsis

A synopsis is the first story vehicle that can be copyrighted, although few people do so. It's more than just an idea, but still much less than a movie. In its practical application, the short synopsis functions more as a marketing tool at the end of the process than as a story-development one at the beginning. Having a short synopsis to circulate is worth as much in the industry as is the architect's first rendering of your future house. It's more about generating inspiration and excitement than giving direction.

Basically, a synopsis is the short summary of your story that contains the sweep of your idea; the theme of the project; and the basic, universal struggle of the main character. It should deliver the piece's scope, tone, and genre, and a sense of its audience.

Here's an example of the short synopsis for the movie *Man of Steel* as it appears on IMDB. This synopsis was written by Warner Bros. Pictures, after the completion of the whole project, and basically for marketing purposes.

> *A young boy learns that he has extraordinary powers and is not of this Earth. As a young man, he journeys to discover where he came from and what he was sent here to do. But the hero in him must emerge if he is to save the world from annihilation and become the symbol of hope for all mankind.*[1]

---

[1] *www.imdb.com/title/tt0770828/plotsummary?ref_=tt_ql_6*

In practice, it really isn't possible to write a short synopsis until the story has been completely broken, a process necessitating a much longer form. However, it can be helpful to writers in an early stage to force themselves to shoehorn the main action of a story into a short paragraph. This format eliminates all the dross and can really reveal whether there is a core of choice-driven action in the story, or just a lot of angst and navel-gazing.

One of the most common documents that may accompany a screenplay when it is sent to production companies is the "one sheet" — essentially a logline and a short, one- or two-paragraph synopsis. A slightly longer synopsis (1–1½ pages) may be created by readers who provide script coverage for production companies and studios. Synopses any longer than two pages are typically considered too long.

c. About a Fiver: Story Proposals

Story proposals are a new hybrid on the development horizon. The authors actually invented this document to use with their clients and students. No document in the general Hollywood arsenal that clearly answered all the basic questions that producers wanted to know about a project before they read a script existed. We also found that we needed a mechanism to get writers to focus on the basic elements that went into a viable visual-story concept before they wrote themselves into a hole.

Many beginners learn the hard way that going to script too soon means re-breaking a story and lots of rewriting. Some scripts cannot be reverse-engineered from their weak storylines, and wind up on the chopping block almost immediately. Many writers waste time and morale writing pages for stories that don't work. It is an act of self-sabotage to write screenplay pages before pulling together all the necessary working elements of a story.

Story is everything. A solid, well-conceived story idea includes all the DNA you need to create your beautiful baby. But if you are missing story elements, your baby will end up looking more like *Battlefield Earth* than *Lawrence of Arabia*. Before writing seventy grueling pages of a story that will never work, run your idea through the following series of tests. You will be able to see right away which parts of your story are well covered, and which are weak or nonexistent.

STORY PROPOSAL

PROPOSED PROJECT TITLE: *How does this title give a sense of your theme, genre, and character?*

LOGLINE: *One emotion-laden sentence that sums up what this movie is about.*

SHORT PITCH: *In one paragraph, tell and sell your story. The following information should be included in a breezy, well-written style.*

- What is the genre of this piece?
- Where does it take place, and in what time period?
- What is the scope of the movie? (i.e., epic studio movie? Quirky indie film? Et cetera.)
- Who will be its primary audience?
- What will make people want to see this movie? How will it be fun / entertaining for the audience? (Think something to learn, something to feel, something to dream about. Think universal truth and spectacle.)

MOVIE THEME: *In one artfully written, arguable sentence, state the main thesis underlying the main character's arc of transformation. You can also include lesser themes in other sentences.*

ARENA: *Describe the unique, entertaining, visual world through which we will dwell in this movie. What will this movie look like on the screen? How will the visuals help set the tone and the theme? If it is a standard location (i.e., courtroom, bar, restaurant, living room, office), describe how this standard location will be presented in a new way in the movie.*

CHARACTER PROFILE: *This section should be at least three pages long.*

- **Characterization:** Age? Intelligence? Education? Worldliness? Financial means? Residence? Appearance? Personal style and quirks? Provide a thorough sense of the way this character is going to look and move on screen.

- **Character:** What is his genius? His charm? What will be missing in the world if he doesn't get his act together? Why will audiences be drawn to him? What are his values, and how did he find them? What would he say he needs most? What stands in his way?

- What are the main conflicts in his life? What are some of the deep paradoxes in his life?

- Who or what is his support system?

- What is his transformational arc in the movie? What leads up to his moment of grace, and does he accept it or not? How is he irrevocably changed at the end of the movie? How is his ending a new beginning?

  SUPPORTING CHARACTER PROFILES: Write at least a paragraph for each of the two or three other principal characters in the piece. Give details of their character and characterizations, and indicate what transformational arc they will travel in the story.

  STORY SYNOPSIS: Divide the main action of the story into acts. This section should be at least five pages.

- **ACT ONE:** Take us through the main action of the first half hour of this movie. Include the way the main character is introduced. Include how you are going to introduce your theme and any visual imagery you will be using. Hook us by indicating the entertaining spectacle in the story that the audience will enjoy. Then, take us through the inciting incident that draws the character into launching the journey of the story by making a choice. Describe the various kinds of conflict that stand in the character's way, including how they are high stakes. Introduce supporting characters and subplots. End with a high-stakes, visual, active choice that puts the character into a new dilemma.

- **ACT TWO:** Take us through the next hour of the film. How does the main character's situation become more complicated? Which of the character's actions drive the story? What changes do we start to see in the arena? Where are the character and his personal relationships in Act Three? What is it that heightens the stakes and suspense? What will continue to make this entertaining for the audience? What is the main reversal that comes at the midpoint? At the end of Act Two, what makes the character's situation as bad as it can be? What is the test that you have set up for the third act?

- **ACT THREE:** Take us through the main action of the third act. What does the main character do? What are the remaining sources of conflict, and how does the character engage them? Where is the character in his relationship in Act Three? How does the character's genius come into play in reaching the resolution of the story? Indicate how you will pay off all your setups. How does the character "die" so as to live? How is the arena changed at the end of the story? What is the new beginning at the end?

Wow, that's a lot of information. If your head is spinning and you don't know where to start, relax. Start with the elements that you already know. Most writers start with a bit of character detail and some story points. Others begin with an interesting arena. Next, take note if there was any part of the proposal on which you came up completely dry. If you didn't even consider your arena, or what your character wants, or the theme of your story, spend some time thinking about those things. Great story ideas take time to flesh out. We promise you: carefully crafting answers for each of these areas before you go to script will save you much more time in the long run.

If you were able to complete the proposal and your story idea passed with flying colors, congratulations! You are ready to pitch your idea to a producer or turn your idea into an outline and get to work. If you already have a draft, try using the proposal as a litmus test to see what areas are working in your script and what areas need more work. We call this "reverse engineering." Not all scripts can be saved; but if it is possible, finding answers to these questions will point the way.

d. About the Cost of Dinner and a Movie: The Beat Sheet

A beat sheet is an "in-house" technical document for writers. It is generally meaningless and incomprehensible to anyone who isn't a writer. In fact, many beat sheets are incomprehensible to anyone *but* the writer who has drawn them up. We've seen beat sheets as simple, two-sheet lists, or as complex graphs with arching lines and lots of notes scribbled in all the white space.

Few producers can make sense of beat sheets. Hence, as consumers who have contracted an elegant-looking screenplay, producers tend to be suspicious of beat sheets and profoundly uninterested in seeing them. A writer who thrusts a beat sheet in front of a producer as proof that work is proceeding is liable to get a raised eyebrow and some kind of a "I don't care; give me screenplay pages" response.

Still, creating a beat sheet may be a good and helpful step for a writer on his or her way to the treatment. A beat sheet focuses on nothing but plot. There is no standard format for a beat sheet. It is a list of the main choices and actions that will constitute the story and form the basis for the structure. A beat sheet is divided into act breaks, and will often have the inciting incident, midpoint, and denouement of the story all set out and labeled clearly. It is helpful in a beat sheet to be able to see the beginning, middle, and end of each of the acts and sequences of the story.

If a story has complementary arcs for two characters, then two beat sheets will probably be required. Overlaying the two should reveal how scenes are going to need to be layered to accommodate both of the characters' journeys.

We have requested beat sheets from our clients and students who really want to write about character or theme, and are either ignoring or struggling mightily with plot. The beat sheet in these cases is a discipline to reign in the writer's self-indulgence and refocus him or her on the plot. If there isn't a plot, there isn't a story. There's nothing for characters to do, and there's nothing to prove or demonstrate a theme.

e. Talking Real Money: The Treatment

Now, we're talking the hard cash of the entertainment business. The treatment may also be called a synopsis (as opposed to a short synopsis), a scene-by-scene, or, for WGA purposes, "The Story." It is generally the result of four to six weeks of the work known in the business as "breaking the story." If the project is a period piece or a research-heavy project, producing a treatment can take three to six months.

Because the treatment is the first story product that is attached to remuneration, whoever produces the treatment is now a stockholder in the new company known as "The Project." If their deal is correctly written, whoever produces the treatment will have a very strong case to get, minimally, a "Story by" credit on the screen.

Unlike the beat sheet, which only focuses on plot, the treatment informs the reader of genre, tone, characters, and all of the other important factors of the story. The treatment does not contain all the artistic flourishes, imagery, or meticulous scene divisions the movie will. Its purpose is to convey a full sense of the story — in broad strokes and employing the same pace and tone that will be used to hook the audience.

The treatment should be single-spaced, and run ten to twelve pages long (or about one page for each ten pages of screenplay). Another way to think of it would be one page for each ten minutes of movie. The writer's name and the project title should be on the header or footer of every page of the treatment right alongside the page number. The treatment should be clearly divided into act breaks with the act headers written out in this manner: ACT ONE, ACT TWO, ACT THREE. Related scenes, sometimes called sequences, can be grouped together in paragraphs so that quickly looking at a page reveals three paragraphs that are the beginning, middle, and end of a ten-minute chunk of the movie. As in a screenplay, character names should be capitalized when introduced as a way of signaling the casting needed for a project.

Except for the act-break divisions, the best treatments are free of technical moviemaking language. Although a treatment is a technical piece from which a producer or director can absolutely discern the timing of a movie story, the piece should read as much as possible like a short story written in engaging and elegant prose.

Generally, treatments go through several rewrites, just like a screenplay. With feature screenplays for budgets of $5 million or more costing nearly $120,000, producers have a right to be very careful about sending a writer to script. But producing a treatment is a good thing for a writer. The advantage of a treatment is that the major story hitches can all get worked out so that time will not be wasted later on when writing the screenplay. A good treatment means a writer will not end up writing down alleys and byways that will just have to be paved over when the story finally comes together. A treatment is an attempt to bring the story together before you have to worry about the artistry and technical requirements of a screenplay.

Sometimes you will hear the term "treatment" used as though it were synonymous with "outline," but there is a distinction. An outline, like the beat sheet, is better used as an internal working document for the writer. It is a fully fleshed-out version of the story which contains all the information on the treatment — plus more thoughts, details, and "notes to self" as they pertain to certain scenes. Depending how detailed the writer chooses to be before going to script, it may be a scene-by-scene document, with lots of notes about the characters' inner and outer journeys. It doesn't need to be pretty or even comprehensible to anyone else. Some writers will turn their treatment into an outline by adding internal notes; conversely, others will extract their treatments from their highly detailed outlines.

As the basic outline for the screenplay, the treatment is not a luxury or in any way gratuitous. It is an essential element of the visual-story process. Writing a treatment is just as key a skill to learn as formatting a screenplay. Woe to the writer who proceeds without one.

CHAPTER 20

THE WRITER'S REAL LIFE

THE NOTES:

- "This writer projects desperation."
- "She always takes a week or more to get back to us."
- "He leaves a touch of resentment with every encounter."
- "This writer seems to have plateaued in her skills."
- "We will need to protect the other people on the team from this writer."
- "I'm so tired of this writer's paranoia."

> *Any man who keeps working is not a failure. He may not be a great writer, but if he applies the old-fashioned virtues of hard, constant labor, he'll eventually make some kind of career for himself as a writer.*
> — RAY BRADBURY

The professional writer's life is marked by its lack of real marks. It is a life without uniform or dress code; without schedule, steady colleagues, or bosses; without regular salary; and generally without an office. Of course, when things are going, you can have all of these — except the uniform — but, on the whole, writers make their living in isolated and largely unseen ways, without any externally imposed structures.

What follows is the list we call "What Comes With the Territory" of being a professional screenwriter. We have compiled the list from the most common complaints and causes of quitting that we have heard from our many students and writing mentees over the years. Tragically, because they haven't taken the time to think ahead about what a writer's real life consists of, many people experience the things on the list as negatives. Really, they are neutral. If you experience these things, it is not that you are necessarily "doing the screenwriter thing" badly. It just means that you are just doing it.

What you need is a strategy to cope with all of the realities of the screenwriting life so that you can turn what might be personal and career stumbling blocks into stepping-stones.

Isolation

> *A creation of importance can only be created when its*
> *author isolates himself; it is a child of solitude.*
> — Johann Wolfgang von Goethe

What you have to sell is not written down anywhere. It doesn't even lie within you for you to just tap into that place and pull it out. The stuff of storytelling is a combination of elements that you pull out of your memory and experience, colored by the wisdom life has given you, dressed up by your imagination, and finally meted out onto paper through your knowledge of the screen art form.

You will be successful in making all these largely spiritual functions work together insofar as you can make yourself retreat into your own head and heart — away from distractions and other voices. You will have to be alone with the blank page, the empty screen, and the quiet room until you are able to fill them up from the store of what is inside you.

Isolation is hard. There is a reason why "solitary confinement" is among the harshest punishments society can inflict upon a criminal. There is no soft-pedaling the reality of having to be by yourself, working for long periods and straining at creativity.

We humans dread isolation because it is boring. Isolation is lonely. Isolation is draining — emotionally, psychologically, mentally, and even physically. An old Italian nun once noted to us that the most exhausting part of her religious life was her annual eight-day silent retreat. "Every year, I think it will be the death of me," she noted with a wry smile.

Finally, isolation can be frightening, because in silence voices that we are running from in our noisy lives very often emerge — voices of remorse or guilt, voices of loss and suffering never dealt with, voices of fear and the memories of humiliation and failure.

There are several ways that isolation or the dread of it gets writers into trouble.

First and foremost, the fear of isolation is what causes writers to procrastinate and avoid starting work at all. Procrastination leads to self-loathing. It sets people into making excuses for why they don't have anything to show for their time, and this just adds to their feelings of guilt. Procrastinators expend tremendous energy in accounting for their failure to get it done. It's their crazy brother-in-law. It's their car that broke down. It's a printer that needs a cartridge, or the local Staples that is out of three-hole paper. It's that the weather was too good or too bad, or that they are suffering from migraines or the flu.

Besides being a source of endless self-loathing and wretchedness, all these protestations amount to is wasted breath. In a very short time, everybody who is working on a project knows everything — so everybody figures out who the folks who just can't deliver are.

Another way that the fear and pressures of isolation causes writers to act out is making them morose, uncommunicative, slovenly, and demanding with friends and family. It can lead a writer to make bad choices just to get a job done, and perhaps even to steal someone else's ideas.

Our strategy for coping with the isolation required for creativity is to turn it into solitude. Isolation means that a writer is alone. Solitude means that a writer has gone off to be alone with Someone. The "Someone" here is God, the Being from whom you draw your being, and Who inspires your creativity regardless of what you call that Being and by what religion you identify yourself.

It is undeniable that writing is a spiritual process. None of us know from where the impulse to connect and create springs, but all of us who are engaged in these tasks have experienced the mysterious muse whimsically descending into our soul, giving us things to say that feel like they come from beyond us. Writers in the zone know that sometimes writing feels like dictation, as though the labors at the craft have suddenly become a doorway into a depth we didn't know we had.

Solitude is a reunion, whereas isolation is a punishment. Solitude is a communion and sharing, whereas isolation is a lone voice that may not make any sense at all echoing off barren walls. Solitude is good and renewing. Isolation is draining. Paraphrasing the Book of Genesis (2:18) in the Bible, "It is not good for the writer to be alone."

Another strategy for coping with isolation is to vigorously balance the time spent working alone with time spent interacting with friends and family. In the same way you have to order yourself to withdraw, you need to order yourself to advance into the company, consolation, and inspiration you can find in other people.

Collaboration

> There is probably no hell for authors in the next world — they
> suffer so much from critics and publishers in this one.
> — C. N. BOVEE

It's ironic that, after isolation, one of the hardest things about being a professional writer is having to work with other people. If you experience any success at all, there will be a point at which your writing becomes a collaborative act. Getting paid to write means that you will have to submit your ideas and projects to others for their notes, feedback, edits, and possibly their rejection.

Being a professional screenwriter means that you will work with many different types of people from every possible background and worldview. You will rarely have a say about with whom you will work. Many times, you will have to collaborate with people who are not as clever or as well educated as you, or as profound or virtuous or as knowledgeable about story and screenwriting.

Producers almost never know as much about screenwriting as writers do. And why should they? Their job has different requirements. It's the writer's job to be the story guru on a project. The writer has to find a way to communicate the essential story and character points in a way that can be heard and internalized by everyone else.

Collaboration can become a stumbling block for writers when it leads them to become overly competitive. It can make a writer feel very pressured to be as good or better than the others on a project. It can make a writer seek out partners in envy or gossip, and can leave people really hating one another.

When collaboration among creative people is good, it's like the antechamber of heaven. It's exhilarating, affirming, exciting, and full of the joy that comes with all those.

When a team of people isn't working well, on the other hand, it is like wading through the fetid, steaming swamp of hell.

In the best and worst times, collaboration can still teach us to be more articulate. Writers need to learn to express essential points of story or art in a clear and compelling way. Collaboration can teach you to be simple and amiable — a grateful presence on the team who always comes into a room like lovely, fresh air through an open window. Instead of being threatened, collaboration should lead you to discover and delight in the mysteries of talent and insight that are in each member of a team.

Our strategy for coping with the necessity of collaboration is to resolve to always be a welcome presence through servitude to all. Someone needs to be the one to make the coffee and clean up the dishes. Why not you? Again, in a short time, everyone knows everything, and everyone wants gracious people on their set. Studiously avoid breaking off into cliques. And never gossip about other members of the team. No, really. Whomever you are venting with is absolutely thinking, "Of course, she talks about me in this same way with other people." It's a bad rap to have. Chances are, you're just not THAT good of a writer that people will want you and your destructive gossip on the next project.

Rejection

Rejection slips, or form letters, however tactfully phrased, are lacerations of the soul, if not quite inventions of the devil — but there is no way around them.
— Isaac Asimov

Being a professional writer means that after you have finally come out of your cave and put your work in front of other people, some of those people will not like it. There is no avoiding this. Success requires that you will have to market yourself in a process Hollywood calls "pitching." Most pitches lead to naught. Again, if you are getting rejected in your efforts as a writer, it doesn't mean that you are doing the writing thing wrong. It just proves that you are doing it, period.

Rejection always hurts. It hurts more than success and validation exhilarate. Looking back at our years as professional writers, we can recall getting notes from producers, mentors, and friends on every script. We can tell you pretty much all the negative notes we got with specificity. But if you ask us what those same people liked about our projects, it all gets very fuzzy. The sting of rejection runs deeper than the thrill of success. But either way, they go together. As long as you might be thrilled by a word of praise, you will have to live with the certainty that the pain of rejection is also out there, just after the next sip of coffee.

Adding to the suffering of rejection is the ironic reality that even most good people are simply awful at rejecting others. It is an innately awkward thing to do — and for anyone with a heart, an even harder thing — because good people tend not to want to hurt others. People tend to avoid hard things, or try to get through them as quickly as possible. This means that rejections tend to come secondhand, or half-assed, or in an abrupt and cursory manner. As with every other part of human life, more messes are made when we are in a rush than in any other circumstance.

Rejection gets writers into trouble by making them depressed and filling them with doubts about their talent and potential. It can make a writer look for validation in inappropriate places, and can make them clingy and needy with friends and family. Rejection makes writers lie and make excuses and assign blame to others. Finally, it can make a writer angry and desirous of revenge.

The hard truth is that there are goods that come into our lives because of failure. If only there was another, better way to learn humility, compassion, empathy, gentleness, and patience! Particularly in this modern era, in which technology seems to be weakening the populace by enabling the avoidance of the simple exigencies of grown-up life, it needs to be stated with clear and absolute conviction: Suffering is not the worst thing that can happen to a person. The loss of integrity is worse. Much worse. The loss of one's soul — as in the ability to sing the distinct song that one was meant to sing — is much worse. Suffering is so much a part of the lives of history's greatest artists that it is safe to say it is actually a mark of great art. The greatest artists always suffer for their very genius, because genius always has a quality of strange freshness that pushes people outside of their comfort zones.

Rejection, once weathered, can make us better human beings. As regards emotional and psychological blows, the best, most compassionate healers are wounded healers. Also, the biggest lessons we have learned tend to have come to us through times of failure. That's just the way things work, and the main reason not to be terrified of rejection. There will be no joy in final achievement if one hasn't experienced the bitterness of failure. As the poet Emily Dickinson noted, "Success is counted sweetest by those who ne'er succeed."

Unfortunately, after the initial and generally paralyzing shock of rejection, the next human response is to lash back. Hence, some of the worst professional mistakes by writers happen in the wake of a rejection. We have seen writers get a tough note and then shoot off a scathing email, completely withdrawing from a project. Generally, this puts them in breach of contract, and then a legal mess that results in all kinds of disasters. Another common case is a writer getting replaced by another writer, and then launching a total war of character assassination on the producer or director. Investors are suddenly getting copied on accusatory emails; people are sniveling on international phone calls; and lawyers are sending "cease and desist" messages to hundreds of people who have no idea what started it all. In the end, investors get spooked and withdraw, projects halt, and people get fired. And all because a writer suffered a blow to his pride.

Our strategy for not being derailed by rejection is first and foremost to expect it; and secondly, not to fear it. The fear of failure causes as many messes as the failures themselves do. Fear of failure makes people shut down and be careful. This is the opposite disposition required to create fresh and bold stories. As the theologian Father James Alberione wrote, "People who live make mistakes. People who surrender to their fears live a mistake."

The key to thriving in a profession in which rejection is just What Comes With the Territory is to have the determination to learn from everything. Every rejection is an arrow of experience in your quiver enabling you to better contribute to life and to show business. A good life as a professional writer does not require that you leap from peak to peak or run without faltering. It just means that you set your jaw and keep on walking. Regardless.

Instability

> *Money is better than poverty.*
> *If only for financial reasons.*
> — WOODY ALLEN

Instability is part of the professional writer's life. Even when there is a series of projects and the pay is good, the work is never regular from year to year. A professional writer will take home a $150,000 payday for a screenplay in one year, and then not have another screenplay sell for the next three years. Or five.

Instability also means that there is almost no constancy in collaborators. A professional writer is a true and thorough entrepreneur — a trawler without a fleet who sails to wherever the fish are. When a project is going, the writer is with the creative team for six months for sixteen hours a day. When the project wraps, the writer may never see those folks again.

This kind of life means that writers can be weirdly available on weekdays, and unable to distinguish weekends from the rest of the week. Writers have time on their hands, until they don't, and then they are stressed and consumed by looming deadlines and the need for absolute focus.

Being a professional writer means no one notices or misses you if you decide not to write today, or this week, or for three months. If you can't self-start projects regardless of whether someone is asking for them, you probably won't be able to pay your rent doing this.

Instability brings stress into a writer's life when it causes him or her to act out in in fear, envy, and jealousy. It can lead a person to treat others like means to an end. It can make a writer sell out or end up very bitter.

Our strategy for coping with the "ons and offs" of a screenwriting career is to do everything you can to write for pay in big and little ways; every writing job makes you better at some skill that will make you a better screenwriter. And as long as you are getting paid for writing, you are living a more whole and consistent life. There should be no snobbery about what kind of writing you will do to keep the instability of the life at bay. In the last twenty years, for example, we two authors have been paid for writing the following:

- Screenplays for features and short films
- Rewrites of other people's screenplays
- Polishes of other people's screenplays
- Industry reviews and features for blogs, websites, magazines, and newspapers

- Script notes and coverage for production companies
- Documentary ideas and scripts
- Ghostwritten speeches for politicians and celebrities
- Copy for press kits
- Web series
- The story for a musical-theater production
- Film-festival program essays
- Book chapters on movies, art, writing, and culture
- Speeches on the same

Secondly, the most successful and peaceful writers in the business have something else to do that provides for their means alongside the writing. We know industry writers who moonlight as business assistants, teachers, development executives, realtors, and staff members at a nonprofit. The best second jobs provide a steady outside source of income without draining the parts of your brain you must conserve for writing. Find a complementary job that can pay your rent and give you a sense of immediate satisfaction while you are making your initial steps as a professional screenwriter. If you start getting so many writing jobs that you need to let something go, you can let go of this "something else." But in the interim, you will have a source of steady income. You will also find that this avocation provides you with a sense of satisfaction, producing immediate results in a way that writing screenplays may never do. One can make a good living writing screenplays that never get made into films, as it were. It can be frustrating.

But the main thing is that you have to learn to cope with the professional screenwriting reality of getting a huge check one day, and then not getting paid again for two years. You have to learn to cope in legitimate ways, and if you — or your spouse — can't find a way to live at peace in this kind of life, chances are you will have to move on to another profession that offers a steady middle-class paycheck and good benefits.

Creative Dilemmas

> *Ethics is knowing the difference between what you*
> *have a right to do, and what is right to do.*
> — Potter Stewart

Being a storyteller is not like working at WalMart. The woman stacking a shelf with deodorant is probably not wrangling inwardly with whether her task is moral and worthy, or whether she will have to answer for it either in court or in eternity.

One of the main things people are paying for in stories is the writer's point of view. This means that a writer needs to put himself out there, choosing what to say and how to say it. Choice implies risk. Risk implies danger. Being a writer means that you have to be up for losing friends and alienating family because of your work. You might lose other jobs. Much, much worse, if you repeatedly make bad choices, you could lose your integrity and self-respect.

What Comes With the Territory of being a professional writer is that — if you are the kind of person who cares about others at all — there will be many more ethical dilemmas that you will have to face than do people in other fields. Your life will mean that you experience a lot more angst than do gas-station attendants. You'll have to worry about compromising too much; and if you do achieve commercial success, you will surely get hate mail from people who think you are corrupting the world. Hollywood is a place where, because the money and influence are great, the stakes can be very high.

Barbara: There will be occasions when you will be pressured to violate your ethics in order to thrive. I remember once being in a room where producers who wanted to buy my script about Emily Dickinson wanted to change Emily into a lesbian. I told them several times using histori-cal evidence that Emily Dickinson wasn't, in fact, a lesbian. It didn't matter. The marketing department at the studio had concluded that the lesbian angle would bring in another $5 million in box office for the project. The head of the development sector waved his hand at me: "We're not making a documentary here."

Ethical dilemmas are always uncomfortable; and again, when people are uncomfortable, they tend to lash out and make messes. Creative dilemmas can cause problems for writers when they spawn frustration and anxiety. They can lead the writer to oversimplify complex matters or seek quick fixes that will only create bigger problems in the end. They can lead a writer to throw up their hands and turn over responsibility for their lives and professional decisions to others.

The good news is: struggling with serious questions makes you a grownup. Big choices form and build character. Ethical dilemmas will tend to make you reach out for good counsel from wiser minds. This will make you a more thoughtful and humble person.

Finally, living in a risky profession means that your life has the potential to be a great adventure. You may not reach the stars, but you won't end up with a handful of mud, either.

Our strategy for coping with creative dilemmas is to build yourself a network of prudent counselors for every aspect of the business. First and foremost, you should have good friends with whom you can talk through situations that are challenging your values. Besides this, at different times you will need a good attorney, a good business manager, several good mentors in the business, and possibly a pastor or spiritual guide.

CHAPTER 21

WORKING WITH A
WRITING PARTNER

THE NOTES:

- **The writer is uneven. She's really good at character, but bad at structure.**
- **Maybe bring someone in to punch up the dialogue?**
- **Lots of good stuff here. Too bad the writer can't spell.**

Demand no more out of your partner than
what you are willing to give yourself.
— MARTHA QUINN

Barbara: *I've worked with writing partners on two projects. Three if you count this book.*

Vicki: *I've done it on one feature, two short films, and two other collaborative story ideas.*

Barbara: *I've recommended partners to several writers because it was clear to me that they were uneven in their skills. I'm going to say chronically uneven. Probably, in the normal course of a career, they would work out their issues in time; but in the immediate moment, they really needed to pair up with someone who could compensate for their problem areas.*

Vicki: *I've seen that the best writing partnerships do have complementary skills. While one party might have more of a left-brained critical-thinking approach, the other might be better at putting together* *abstract ideas or developing characters. Where one might be good at structure, the other is good at story.*

When writing partnerships go well, there is a mutual respect and admiration for what the other person brings to the table.

Barbara: *They actually teach each other, so that the writer who started weak in character, as the partnership progresses, becomes stronger. It seems the main reason to make this step.*

Vicki: *It can be very motivating to work together. It breathes new life into a project; and with partnerships, you are looking at the same page with different perspectives.*

Barbara: *It's like producing the rewrite while you're actually only on the first draft, because the partners will see the flaws that usually remain hidden to someone working alone.*

Vicki: *There is instant feedback.*

Barbara: *You also can't discount the sheer joy and fun of working with someone —*

Vicki: *Like Vicki. [laughs uproariously]*

Barbara: *[clears throat] It's just a lot of fun to work on something when you are both talented and trained and have a measure of experience. You're doing something that, in the global perspective, not a lot of other people know how to do. And it's coming together. I remember laughing my head off when I worked on a collaborative comedy project. And on our drama project, we were both feeding off each other's intensity.*

Vicki: *There is an instant validation that comes from working together. Often we work alone, and we don't really know how the words are going to be received. But with a writing partner there is instant approval. There is an immediate sense that what we have here is good, and that can be very empowering.*

Barbara: *You also can't understate the human-respect factor that comes to the fore when working with a partner. On my own, I may or may not get my writing done this week. But when I know there is a partner waiting for those pages, someone I respect and whose respect I'd like to keep, it's amazing how motivated I am to do my work.*

Vicki: There's built-in accountability in working with someone. It's a lot harder to slink off to play a few rounds of Words With Friends — unless both partners end up procrastinating together! Especially when you're in the breaking-the-story phase, just being able to talk it out with someone is hugely valuable. You can go through so many bad ideas, get them out, and move past them to the good ones in a way that you just can't sitting alone in a room staring at a blinking cursor.

Barbara: As each partner vets her ideas, the other partner really stands in for the audience in that way. The reactions and responses of the partner can immediately reveal if something is working or not.

Vicki: I guess we should talk about the dark side, too. There can be several factors that cause writing partnerships to collapse or not really be worth the effort. One can be that the relationship actually spawns a sense of competition instead of collaboration. Another would be if, instead of coming together and delighting in each other's gifts, the partners end up focusing on each other's faults. That partnership will soon fall apart.

Barbara: Seems like the first test of how it is working is whether it is making your life as a writer more productive or not. If the partnership is adding stress to your life instead of ameliorating it, you should rethink the arrangement.

Additionally, there are higher stakes in a partnership than going it on your own. When a professional writing partnership goes south, it's more than just a friendship potentially being lost. There are always legal complications that can be nightmarish. Who owns what? How do you split ideas and concepts that have been mutually worked out? Who is going to get the credit on what? My experience has been that the projects just have to die along with the partnership.

Vicki: Whenever there is money or ego or credit on the table that needs to be shared with another, it will be a sticky situation. People can go in with the best of intentions; but if they aren't really clear about expectations, then it can make for a real mess with a lot of acrimony in the bargain.

Barbara: *If at the end, one partner is not willing to just say, "You take it; I'll step back," then chances are the whole thing will dry up. It's like Solomon judging the two women with the baby.*

Vicki: *If you're considering getting into a partnership with someone, here are some topics that you should discuss together. First, what do we each bring to the table? And, if there is overlap —*

Barbara: *As there will be —*

Vicki: *Right — how will we manage that? The next question is: What is your style as a writer, and how do you like to write? What are the logistics? Are we going to be writing in the same room? Will we be trading off our pages and doing rewrites on them? Will we each take scenes and then cut and paste them together?*

Barbara: *A lot of the process issues will evolve as the relationship progresses. But the fundamental question — What is the main value of us joining together? — needs to be clearly answered by both sides. There needs to be a clear reason on each side for making a partnership, and both parties need to know those reasons. That way, each can be sure they are meeting the other's expectations.*

Vicki: *Sometimes people end up working together just because they are thrown together and they want the mutual support.*

Barbara: *So the whole reason for merging comes down to something as simple as, "You're fun, and we laugh together, and writing a screenplay is hard and lonely, so I'd rather work with you than be on my own"?*

Vicki: *It happens.*

Barbara: *I think that could be legitimate; but as soon as either or both achieve any success, or make other relationships, expect that partnership to dissolve. But it needs to be very clearly articulated in the beginning. If that motive isn't mutual, then it is unlikely that both parties will sign on. Both parties need to agree that, "We are using each other equally here."*

Vicki: *Newly partnered writers often believe that they can "figure this out together."*

Barbara: *Which is fine. But there will come a day when they will have figured it out, and now the partnership needs a new reason to continue.*

You really want to ensure early on that the partnership incorporates a way of assessing how everything is going, like an informal set of benchmarks and goals for progress on a project. Then, if one party wants to tweak things or get out, it won't be as shocking or traumatic to have "The Talk."

Vicki: *I think it goes back to respect and communication. Treating one another with respect for what each adds to the equation — and clear, honest, and humble communication if there is anything lacking in the partnership. It could be something as simple as regularly asking each other, "What can we do better?"*

Barbara: *I'm recalling a partnership of two friends I knew where there was a fundamental misconception between them that caused lot of strife. One partner saw the partnership as a sharing of the work. The other saw it as a way to produce double the amount of work. This was a biggie. It's probably never a good idea in a field this demanding to be looking for ways to be less rigorous. Even in a partnership, you have to work as much as one person working alone.*

Vicki: *You still need a lot of grace and flexibility, because you don't get your own way all of the time. The way that a project develops with a partner can sometimes feel slow because you are waiting for feedback from another person.*

Barbara: *That can be frustrating when you think you know the way you want to go. But it is part of your commitment to submit your creativity to this joint process.*

Vicki: *The ultimate litmus test for whether the partnership is working is whether the project itself flourishes —*

Barbara: *More than whether the partners do!*

Vicki: *Yup.*

CHAPTER 22

WORKING WITH PRODUCERS

THE NOTES:

- "Where is she? We said 11:30, right?"
- "What is this? This is nothing like what we talked about!"
- "I don't need excuses. I need pages!"
- "I don't think we want the writer and our star in the same room together."

Everyone always wants to know how to get their work to agents. The truth is, nobody knows. The way agents acquire clients is much more about poaching them from lower-level managers and attorneys than it is about being hooked by the clever schemes of savvy writers.

It's much easier to get your work in front of producers than agents. And how does one do that? Um, nobody knows. But it is easier. Really.

Sigh.

It's the terrible, awful paradox of this business: Everyone needs good scripts, but everyone has built thick walls around themselves to keep writers away. There are reasons for this, of course. Mainly the reason nobody wants to look at a new writer's work is that, for too long, millions of people who weren't writers have been writing scripts and glutting all the channels of the industry with ill-conceived, badly executed, "this is a complete waste of my time" projects. It makes all of us who read scripts professionally very cagey.

But say you do have a project that demonstrates that you know what you are doing as a writer. You have a better chance breaking in by winning over a producer than an agent. First of all, there are many more producers in the entertainment world than agents. Agents actually need training and certification. They have legal boundaries to their profession. But anybody with a hammer can put a shingle with the title "producer" on their house.

Also, by the time someone makes it up to the level of a real agent, the years of juggling high-stakes deals, absurdly complex contracts, monumental egos, and big paychecks have rendered them very jaded and circumspect. They tend to only be interested in the imminent deal, and not in cultivating the longtime, iffy prospect. And who can blame them? As a commission-based career, agents must focus on the clients who bring in money.

On the other hand, because there is a new producer emerging every five seconds, it is possible to find one who is still starry-eyed about the business, who has a fistful of cash, and who has a lot more dreams than knowhow. Inexperienced writers need to build relationships with producers of all kinds who might be their entryway into the business, but the most accessible producers also happen to be new. Nobody wants to be the first one to hire a new writer. The ones most often willing to take chances on them are new producers.

a. How Does a Writer Meet Producers?

Internalize the notion that show business is mainly an entrepreneurial venture. Even the people with jobs at studios, networks, and production companies tend to always be on the alert for an opening at any other studio, network, or production company that would mean more clout, money, or opportunity for them. Writers and actors are the least stable of all the hungry, competitive characters in this business. The game of getting the next gig never ends.

There is no clear path when it comes to seeing one's film make it to the screen, and no two paths look the same — but there are common variables. The first jobs a writer gets will usually be through friends who are also neophytes in the business. Newbies work with their friends because only friends will work for the fun of it and for paltry pay.

Born out of inexperience, idealism, and very little financing, newbie projects tend to become cautionary tales of financial loss and hard lessons learned. They generally produce unwatchable disasters that do not go beyond the family and friends of the folks who labored on them. The main thing you want as a writer in these experiences, aside from valuable insight about the process, is to be able to emerge saying, "I got paid something — even just a little bit — to write that." It's a delight, of course, if the project actually has some good in it and gets noticed. Every once in a while, a project will "break out" and exceed everyone's expectations, but that is far more the exception than the norm.

The kinds of projects to which new writers should be adding their talents include: short films, documentaries, public-service announcements, used-car commercials, the intros and copy for Electronic Press Kits (EPKs) — pretty much anything at all that requires words. All of it is writing, and all of it keeps you in contact with people who are producing projects. No one enters show business to write the text for EPKs. But scores of people who are working on EPKs today will be working on $100 million studio features tomorrow. It's the way of the business. What writers need to do is join the "friend list" of everybody around them doing this stuff; one day, they will call you out of the blue because they need a writer.

Once a writer has gotten their first few jobs out of the way, other work should start to appear mysteriously. If people like you, they end up mentioning you to other people they know. Many artists want to provide others with good crew in the hopes that the favor will be returned when their next project rolls around and they are in need. It's the kind of favor that always pays off and comes back around in a good way. The rule is to take every meeting for as long as you can. Once your career acquires momentum, you can consider being choosier about meetings; but even then, it is better to listen and pass graciously than just turn down a meet and greet.

Most writing jobs are "on assignment." This means that a producer is looking for a writer to execute a project which they already have in mind. They are trying to find a writer to align with their vision of the project. This is a completely different situation than selling a spec script, which is your own original material. It means that you will need to produce one or two writing samples that will place you in contention for the particular project the producer has already lined up.

Writers ought to have either a handful of solid specs that cover several genres and tones, or a handful of specs that carve out a particular niche. Think about your skills and how you want to be branded as a writer. Are you a strong, all-around writer, or are you the "quirky comedy" guy or the "psychological thriller" guy? In your specs, aim for a couple of small-scope movies and one much larger.

b. How to Know If a Producer Is a Good Fit for You

Successful relationships between writers and producers start with the things that make any kind of professional collaboration work: mutual respect, trust, openness, fairness. The fact that so many creative people struggle to make these relationships successful generally comes down to a dearth of these qualities in the ranks of show business overall. Because they live in a world of self-promotion and personal hype, creating the illusion of success, and luring investors — which are both very important skills for the job — showbiz producers often have the ethics of used-car salesmen.

If you have certain values, you cannot expect everyone with whom you work in show business to share them. That is an unrealistic expectation that will limit your career and basically render you unhirable in most situations. Other than writing the best story possible, writers hold very little responsibility regarding what else happens in or around the project.

Our advice to beginning writers is to give most new producers a bit of leeway. As we noted, bringing together a project invariably means hype; and as long as it doesn't go over the line into serious distortion and deceit, a writer can be indulgent about a producer's enthusiasm.

A red flag is an out-and-out lie. If happenstance permits you to find out that you are being lied to before anything is locked in, you should run, not walk away, from the deal. The principle is: "Liars lie. Cheaters cheat." If someone lies to you in the early stages of a project, when the stakes are low, they will lie to you throughout the process. Eventually, when the stakes are high, you will be left standing in the rain, with a sick look on your face, trying to figure out what just happened. Lying producers seldom have successful track records in the business anyway — which makes it a pleasure to avoid them. The best producers also happen to be the most reliable, straight-dealing, on-time, on-budget people in the business. They are rare, but they do exist.

Here is some information to gather about a particular producer before making a formal deal. Each of these can lead to one red flag or another:

- Does the producer have money in hand (Enough to produce a movie? Develop a movie? Pay a writer?), or is he making big promises about funds not yet secured?
- What has she previously produced?
- Who does he really know to get this project made?
- What do others say about her?

- Has he lied to you yet?
- Does he want you to work without a contract?
- Is she making promises about future projects?
- MOST IMPORTANTLY: Do you feel comfortable with him?

Creatively, you can tell if a producer is a good fit for you if any of his or her projects match your tone and style. If you write fantasy-action stories and the producer has only made a series of intense issue dramas, chances are you are going to have different ideas about what excellence in a screenplay means. Ask the producer to give you a script they have on their slate that shows what they like. If you can see yourself writing something that will similarly please the producer, you should consider the job.

c. Parameters of a Working Relationship

Too many writers and producers get into trouble because each side has unrealistic expectations about the other's role. Writers tend to want producers to have an artistic appreciation of cinema and to understand the nuances of the screenwriting craft. Typically, producers don't know or care about these things, which is why they hire writers in the first place. The job of a producer requires juggling the script, casting, finance, investors, scheduling, and any number of other elements. Any one of these (or many) can come crashing down at any time without notice.

Producers tend to want writers to be as passionate as producers are about selling a piece. They want writers to be irresistible "in the room," or at least not completely embarrassing!

Writers want to take the time to get the story stuff right. Producers want to get the money and get the show on the road.

Here follows the stages and correct expectations of the producer/ writer relationship on a hypothetical project.

1. **The Meet and Greet** — An absolutely crucial, sacred, and generally amiable Hollywood ritual, this first face-to-face sit-down between the writer and producer (or agent / manager /

development exec) is either the doorway into a new working relationship, or just a free lunch (or maybe only a cup of coffee) for a writer. The producer might have some other project members from his or her team in attendance as well.

The purpose of the meet and greet is for both parties to get a look at each other. There is usually a lot of lighthearted banter about sports, or recent trips back home, or any kind of stir in pop culture. Both parties are scoping for chemistry and trying to determine (without actually outright asking) things like, "Do I like you? Could I trust you?"

Eventually, the meet and greet gets around to the project and the producer's vision for it. The producer might pose perceived challenges in executing the project as a script, and ask the writer how he or she might handle those. The back and forth here is geared towards both parties discerning if a creative marriage can occur. Do we sync in the way that we communicate and, more importantly, in our sense of the story?

Generally, right before this meeting, the writer has provided a sample of his work to the producer that demonstrates his or her ability to take on this new project. It's assumed that you're in the room because the producer already likes your writing.

Writer's Role and Expectations: The writer should:

- Offer as honest assessment as is possible of his readiness to take on and execute this new project.
- Give a thoughtful sense of how he sees the story in terms of genre, scope, and tone.
- Provide a realistic, approximate timetable to complete the script, or at least the first few stages of it.
- Expect that the producer has funds in place to pay for a script, and has secured any necessary rights to the project.

Producer's Role and Expectations: The producer is the potential employer in this encounter, and is the primary servant and protector of the fundamental project vision. He should:

- Give the writer as strong a sense as possible as to what the tone and rating of the piece should be, the parameters of the budget, and any other limits that might be in place on the story.
- Put faith in the writer's good-faith assessments of both their professional track record and of the time it will take to complete the screenplay.
- Ask for additional writing samples and professional recommendations, if he wants them.

2. The Deal — The hard reality is, even when there is a rock-solid, attorney-negotiated, WGA-registered deal papered, people still get into terrible conflicts over movie projects. Part of the problem is that creativity has a mysterious aspect that is impossible to codify and structure according to the parameters and language of a legal agreement.

Most writers cringe at the idea of pursuing arbitration and litigation. As "creatives," "legal stuff" is often far from our list of strengths and talents. However, if you sign a contract, you have to be prepared to understand and defend that contract — whatever it takes.

Writer's Role and Expectations: It's normal to feel nervous about signing on to write a script. But you have to know what a professional screenplay will mean, and feel confident that you can deliver one.

So, if you aren't a member of the WGA and are just starting out, how much should you charge? A good, basic set of guidelines are:

- Start at **10% below WGA** minimums (until you are in the Guild). Refer to the Schedule of Minimums for current rates.
- A modest amount of money up front is almost always better for the writer than large amounts promised later. If they want to defer full payment, a nice bonus should be negotiated.
- Financing bonuses are better than production bonuses. Both are better than "back end" bonuses.

There are many factors that go into contracts. Regardless of whether you have an agent, it is always wise to hire an entertainment attorney to write up and / or review your deal.

Producer's Role and Expectations: Once a fair deal is reached, the producer has a right to expect the writer to be as dedicated to the project as possible; to be passionate, rigorous, and disciplined; and to keep development matters confidential. Producers constantly battle time and money. They need to keep the writer's costs and schedule on track, and at the same time, provide the writer with the time and opportunity to do the job right.

Invariably, when producers succeed in convincing writers to make bad deals, it comes around and bites the whole project in the ass. An unhappy writer who feels used will lack enthusiasm and rigor in the execution of their job. It isn't worth it to save a couple of thousand dollars, and may cost the project an excellent, complex, and beautiful script.

3. The Write — A writer is expected to deliver a screenplay in three phases: a write, a rewrite, and a polish. The write phase is the most exciting and nerve-wracking phase. We are finally going to stop dancing around and get down to work. The movie is actually going to materialize.

The writer is nervous during the write because screenwriting is hard and complex, and a beautiful screenplay is always a nearly impossible task. The producer is nervous because he or she has taken a chance on a writer, and there is no guarantee that their hunch was right until the pages start coming in. Also, while the writer is working away, the producer is busy. Chances are, a whole mountain of deals are now in place, all riding on the screenwriter's ability to deliver on time and brilliantly. See the section on treatments for the initial expectations for a writer on a project.

Writer's Role and Expectations: A writer is expected to deliver a screenplay three times, with each draft getting closer to the perfection for which everyone on the team is hoping. Each draft should be of the highest professional quality. A "first draft" turned in to the producer is often the fifth or sixth actual draft. After each phase is delivered, the producer gets a chance to disseminate the script to associates and readers and receive notes.

It is the writer's job to give producers what they want. Sometimes, the producer will be happy with things that go against a writer's best instincts in terms of craft. Make the case where appropriate; but in the end, give them what they want.

The rewrite should take into account all the serious notes, and also address some cosmetic notes involving arenas, subplots, and supporting characters.

The polish should be all about adding delight and artistry to the piece. It should address any technical and line notes, solidify the theme, and ensure that every part in the project would make for a fun and meaty role for an actor.

Producer's Role and Expectations: Generally, a producer's notes on the write should broadly cover plot, character, structure, genre, and tone. The notes on this phase are critical, because the producer has the right to demand a full-scale revamp of the script for the rewrite.

Because note-giving is so critical, it is the producer's role to either master this science, or to retain someone who can communicate notes in a way that a writer can understand.

It is the producer's role to believe in and fully support the writer who he or she has hired. The time for discernment is over, and the writer needs to be embraced as a key part of the team. Everyone needs to be committed to finding a way to help the writer get the script where it needs to be. The producer needs to be a master of tough love with the writer: understanding and sympathetic, but holding the line on deadlines and budgets. Be clear without being brutal. Be open to the writer who has discovered a better way to go. Be lavish and specific with praise where it is deserved, and be careful about criticism that could paralyze.

The producer has a right to expect the writer to be a grownup when receiving hard notes. The producer shouldn't have to fear that the writer might fold under criticism or become petulant or depressed. The producer has a right to expect the writer to be a professional.

Timelines are more often dictated by budget and casting than common sense, but a reasonable basic timeline for completing a feature screenplay might be:

- *Research / note gathering (2–3 months)*
- *Location visit (optional) (1–2 weeks)*
- *Full treatment (1 month, then meet and pitch)*
- *Reworking the story (2 weeks, then meet and pitch)*
- *First draft (3 months)*
- *Wait for producer's notes (1 month)*
- *Rewrite (6 weeks)*
- *Wait for producer's notes (2 weeks)*
- *Polish (2 weeks)*
- *= roughly 11 months*

4. Development and Production — After a script is delivered, the next phase of project development involves attracting the money, talent, and collaborators to get the movie done. Because oftentimes no one knows the script and story as well as the writer, the producer may want to bring the writer in to meet investors, actors, and studio reps. Sometimes, producers will have media-oriented events geared to raising awareness of the project.

Writer's Role and Expectations: The job of the writer at this phase is to be as helpful as possible to the producer by being charming, thoughtful, and enthusiastic about the project. This is the time for writers to suppress their weird, artistic impulses and not be any kind of headache for the producer. The producer will have other people already providing headaches. The writer needs to be very aware of that.

A lot of the work that a writer will be asked to do at this phase will be uncompensated. Do it anyway. In the end, everyone wants the same thing: to assemble the resources for the script to be produced. If the movie goes, every little hour spent schmoozing and promoting it will be worth it.

Producer's Role and Expectations: If a writer has behaved well, delivered on time, and produced a good screenplay, a producer should treat him or her with a kind of reverence. The writer should be part of promotion efforts, and should be on the red carpet if the project goes all the way. Just saying. Beyond that, a producer should keep the writer at the table as long as possible in deference to his or her invaluable contribution to the project. Mindful that the writer is an entrepreneur, the producer should recommend the writer for other projects.

Finally, the producer is responsible for providing all of the writer's residuals and interests as a constituent member of the team. The writer should not have to have the WGA come calling on the producer.

CHAPTER 23

STUDIO VS. INDIE:
WHERE DOES YOUR PROJECT FIT?

THE NOTES:

- "This is an art-house movie, but it doesn't take enough risks."
- "Where's the star role?"
- "We don't know how to market this."
- "It's good, just too quirky for us."
- "The scope is too small."
- "The scope is too big."

American storytelling — movies, TV, music, books, and software — ranks among the largest U.S. exports, which, in turn, feeds a global industry. It's a *huge* multibillion-dollar business with many moving parts. While stories still fuel the human need to know oneself and connect through shared experiences, modern-day screen storytelling is powered by commercialism. The storyteller's material must be commercially viable in order for it to find an audience. The writer has to have a sense of how and why it is going to sell, as much as what the primary conflict is and where the first act will end. The storyteller might only be interested in the latter, but it is the former that gets their story seen around the world. Likewise, businesspeople in entertainment might have all the formulas to make money, but it is the fundamentals of good storytelling that still make or break every project.

All through the creative process, a writer should have a project's ultimate distribution always nagging at their mind. Having an idea where you will find the best audience for your project will absolutely impact story choices. How do you know if you are writing a studio project or a little gem for the festival circuit? What makes for mass appeal, and what is the stuff of a critical darling?

The Studio Route

Studio movies are typically big-budget, popcorn-selling, movie-star-driven vehicles. While some companies, like Disney / Pixar, have an excellent, collaborative development process that consistently turns out great stuff, it's more common for the result to reek of there being too many chiefs and not enough Indians. The top-heavy nature of a studio often translates to too many agendas. Studio execs struggle to rein in unwieldy projects. While there are a limited number of "Written by" credits on a movie, dozens of uncredited writers may be brought into the process, creating a muddy mess of a story.

We once met a writer who had a project completely gutted by her producer in concert with a studio development executive. Basically, the studio had demanded that the project come in at $10 million less than the budgeted amount. The project was cut and slashed by a group of studio lawyers, MBAs, and publicity people to lose a full twenty pages (and thirty minutes of screen time). Then, months later, the writer was called back in and told that no one understood the story anymore, so she should, "Please fix the problems, but don't add any more pages." When the writer protested that she should have been in on the edits of the original script, she was told by the producer, "We thought about it, but then we knew you would say, 'Story, story, story' — and we didn't have time for that."

Studios are sequel machines, but occasionally an original screenplay will make it through. So why would anyone put their beloved, cohesive, and brilliant screenplay through this? Money. And fame. It's like winning the lottery. Even if you aren't being driven by the bigger payday, some projects still take a lot of money to execute. If your story is big and epic, or very clear in a genre that brings in large audiences, you will need studio support. Bigger budgets mean a bigger cut for the writer. Getting paid mid-six figures doesn't stop you from knowing they screwed up your story, but it is a big consolation. A studio release is prestigious. It means your project's star will be on *The Today Show* opining about what the piece means to the world. It means you will get interview requests from Australia and Italy, and an invitation to the premiere in Seoul. It means that millions of people will see your movie.

A feature film that works its way through the studio system tends was likely first developed by larger, more established production companies. "More established" here means that the production company has a track record of projects that have made money. They have worked with big budgets and big stars and they have relationships or even "first-look deals" at major studios. Because people tend to buy what they like, many of these established production companies have a distinct brand of product. Some examples include Focus Features (*Lost in Translation, Eternal Sunshine of the Spotless Mind, Traffic*); Touchstone Pictures (*Pretty Woman, Armageddon, Sister Act*); or Newmarket Films (*The Passion of the Christ, Donnie Darko, Memento*).

A writer with a project that will require a lot of money and mainstream distribution first needs to get a hearing at one of these larger production companies. Very often, one way to do so is by forging a relationship with a smaller production company who will then bring the project up the line to the large entity with the studio deal. This is why movies very often have credits that list several production companies, as in "A Weird Little Company Film in association with A Pretty Big Production Company in a film by A Major Studio."

When a large production company brings a project to a studio, the studio's development executives immediately begin developing input on the story and style of the project to maximize profits.

Studios have fairly reliable formulas to tell them how much money they can make if they have a certain star in a film, opening on a certain weekend, and based on name-recognition material. Most studio movies these days are made from preexisting material, which already has a built-in audience or fan base. It is easier for a studio to predict how much box-office yield will come from *Batman 27!* than from a fresh, original idea.

This has huge consequences for a writer. It's very difficult to get a hearing at a large production company for an expensive and completely original story. They don't want it because it will be a hard sell at a studio. The only way to assure a hearing is to come to the production company with most of the budget already raised.

What this means for the screenwriter who writes studio movies is that they will often be pitching their take on a preexisting story idea for the purpose of being hired to write the movie. Studio writers have professional samples of their original ideas which are just as high concept as the writing in the finished big-studio movies (and usually better executed) — but these usually exist to land the writer additional work. Studio writers are proven, which means they have written something else which has yielded box-office results.

The Independent Route

An "independent" film is one that gets made outside of the studio system. If these projects are any good, they generally get picked up and distributed by a studio, which is the dream goal of most every independent producer. Every studio has their own "independent" arm, and is always on the hunt for "little gems" which can be acquired for a few million and then yield triple or quadruple their investment through marketing to a niche audience.

An independent-film budget is generally much lower than a studio film. They tend to be much murkier in genre, often mixing and merging subgenres. Whereas a studio film could be described as a "big-budget action movie," an indie is more often a combination like a "psychological thriller / sci-fi picture with gothic themes and offbeat romance." (Okay, we're exaggerating. Please don't send us *that* script.)

Indies are very often passion projects and represent the kind of original storytelling that is completely gone from the studio development world. Because budgets are small, indie films generally incorporate a lot of artistic experimentation to aid the storytelling. Or they may eschew special effects altogether in favor of small-canvas, quirky, character-driven tales. Real actors tend to love indie movies because they afford the opportunity to really go in new directions and try out strange things that would never get by a studio. An example would be gorgeous Charlize Theron grossing herself up to play a serial killer in *Monster* — a role which won Theron an Oscar.

From a writer's standpoint, the indie route means that you have far fewer people to please. Even if a studio does eventually take over the project, the movie is already in the can. They can ask for some scenes to be cut or edited, but they can't tinker too much with the story.

Even so, in order for an indie to get any kind of distribution, it must meet many of the same demands of a studio movie. It still needs a star to "sell" the movie. It still needs a "hook," or something that no one has seen before. It needs to feel "fresh" yet "commercial." Even though indies are far more experimental than studio films, they can't stray too far from the conventions of Hollywood. Movies that do well at the major film festivals, like Sundance, still struggle to secure distribution, and distribution is very much tied to what yields a higher return.

Where studios suffer from too many chiefs, indies suffer from not enough of them. Sometimes there's no one on the producing team giving the critical notes necessary to keeping the story and director in check. One of the biggest mistakes we see with film-makers on the indie track is that they are so passionate to make their movie that they take dangerous risks, such as mortgaging their home, because they are overconfident about their untested, unproven material. In the end, all indie producers still need to prove, at least on paper, that there is an audience for their movie in order to convince investors to fund it. Indies are still dependent on "high-concept" material that will draw crowds.

Micro-budget Filmmaking

Because of the advancement of technology, micro-budget movies are an exciting new way for filmmakers to break in. A micro-budget film is typically crowd-funded (i.e., by family and friends) or financed through a single investor. The assumption is that everyone is working for (nearly) free, and that in order to get the film made funding need only cover the absolute bare minimum expenses.

For the screenwriter, that means that you're writing for almost nothing, or for deferred pay based on any back-end profits (which you shouldn't expect). Stories that do well on the micro-budget level have ideas that are visceral and universal, and are uniquely matched to the unpretentious style of a project that lacks money. Think of *The Blair Witch Project*. These films will generally be shot in a few standard locations, mostly interiors, and will rely much more on acting chops than a truly cinematic experience. Their success is dependent on the film either going viral online or winning big at festivals, which might attract distributors.

While there might be little financial risk in getting this type of film made, the odds of a micro-budget film truly breaking out and competing at the level of bigger movies are slim, which means the audience will only ever be very small. However, if one's goal is to build credits and gain some hands-on experience, this is a viable way for a new screenwriter to see their story on screen.

CHAPTER 24

NETWORKING

THE NOTES:

- "Never heard of her."
- "If he'd stop acting so desperate, maybe he'd have a chance."
- "We don't know if we want to take a chance on her."
- "This writer doesn't care about relationships. He's just using people."
- "The writer seems to be trying to tell me what I want to hear."

> *I don't want to belong to any club that will accept people like me as a member.*
> — GROUCHO MARX

Writing movies is something anyone can do anytime they want. Making movies is about who you know. Or rather, who knows you.

Networking is a vital part of a screenwriter's career. Movies are a collaborative medium, and how a writer connects with other collaborators is as important as what a writer can deliver on the page. People naturally want to work with people with whom they have a bond of experience and trust. It's rare to find someone with whom you jibe creatively and personally. That's the reason why Tim Burton and Johnny Depp, or Steven Spielberg and John Williams, or Martin Scorsese and Leonardo DiCaprio team up over and over again.

Many writers tell us they don't like to network because it makes them feel cheap and smarmy. They hate "schmoozing" their way through a party or a premiere. They'd rather be judged by their brilliant writing than by how good they are in a room. They are deep thinkers; they don't like being artificial and fake. If you've ever felt that way when networking, we have some advice for you:

Stop being artificial and fake.

Effective networking means building genuine and lasting relationships with others. It means you really get to know and value the people around you. It means you are a good listener. You are dependable. You are trustworthy. You care about who a person is, not what he or she can do for you. You are a Real Human Being.

It's rare, but lovely when we come across Real Human Beings in this business. When we do, they become true friends, and we want to help them whenever and however we can. We may not always have an immediate opportunity for them, but we are always on the lookout should something come up. Successful writers in Hollywood know many, many people, and all of those relationships are valuable. However, only a few of those relationships might become a connection for employment.

Most often, a writer's first "break" isn't going to come from a Hollywood bigwig. It's going to come from one of his peers with whom he's watched the Super Bowl or climbed Mount Baldy. Our friend, writer / producer David McFadzean, says he got his first break because he slept with his producer, Matt Williams... not *that* way, but as college roommates! They went on to create the hit TV show *Home Improvement*, and have worked together for over thirty years.

When we speak to incoming classes of writers and producers, we tell them to look around the room; it's not the faculty or visiting speakers from Hollywood who will likely offer them a job, but their peers. When one peer makes it, she brings as many friends along with her as she can. It takes a lot of acquaintances to turn into friends like these. So how do you find them?

Go to School

You don't necessarily need an advanced degree to write screenplays, but you do need the equivalent in professional training and practice. The other benefit of an academic or professional program is access to a community of people who are serious about the craft. Many alumni from top film schools succeed because of the networks in place at the major studios and production companies. Your fellow students are the people with whom you want to start building relationships. If you show promise as a writer and a Real Human Being, you may also be noticed by faculty who want to help you.

But even the small group of writers at the local university extension program can yield a couple new friends who are going to find a way into the business. If people are making an investment in learning the craft, chances are that they are going to take a serious shot at a career.

Get a Job

It's widely known that working as an assistant in Hollywood is a great way to be positioned for bigger opportunities. The Catch-22 for many assistants who are aspiring writers is that they have day jobs that demand so much from them that they don't have time to write! If you can hold down an assistant job and hang in there as a writer, the day will come where your connections will pay off. Other good, foot-in-the-door jobs include working in the mailroom at a major agency, or temp work at any of the major studios. Hollywood hires from within, and no job is too small if you're trying to break in. If you do really good work and meet people's needs, you will move up.

Of course, you will have a happier life if you treat every person well on your way up. But it will also mean that you will have a more successful professional life. Many people who work for decades in Hollywood eventually find themselves being offered a job by someone they hired once years ago.

Join a Professional Organization

There are many great organizations in Hollywood designed specifically for meeting people and building relationships. They aren't shy about calling it "networking" for the purposes of getting ahead, but it's still done by being a Real Human Being. Some of the best organizations offer mentoring, which is a fabulous way to gather advice from the wise sages of Hollywood. So check out Women in Film, or the International Animation Association, or Cinema for Peace, or the various industry academies. If you want to meet people who are making movies, you need to be friends with people who love movies.

Go to Parties

Old Hollywood did it best, making deals in pool halls and card rooms. The good ol' boys clubs of the past still meet today — although generally half the people in the room are women, thank God! We're in the entertainment business, so being able to relax and enjoy oneself in this highly competitive, stress-inducing field is essential to personal and professional growth. If you're no fun to be around, guess what? Hollywood doesn't want to be around you.

Make the Most of Your Location

It's true that people who live in Hollywood have an embarrassment of riches when it comes to networking opportunities. If you don't live in Hollywood, there are other ways of building relationships. Find the local film chapter. If your town has a film festival or a film commission, get to know the people involved. There are online networking groups for you to join. Independent film is thriving outside of Hollywood (as well as inside), so if that's your thing, living outside of Hollywood is no excuse for you.

Turn Off the Computer

Many writers turn to social networking to "get out there," seldom with good results. Unless you have a face-to-face rapport with a real, live person, your cyber relationship won't allow the kind of deep connection we're talking about. Many people incorrectly assume that being Facebook friends with a successful writer or director and seeing them in their newsfeed means they suddenly have claim to ask for favors. Just don't.

It's a turnoff to people in the business to receive pitches on social networks if they've never met the person face-to-face. Remember, you are a Real Human Being, and so is the person you want to meet. Get to know them in an authentic way.

CHAPTER **25**

SUCCESS

The Notes (from a writer's POV):

- **"What if I never make it?"**
- **"They like me! They really, really like me!"**
- **"I made it. Why don't my friends like me anymore?"**
- **"She made it. She's so full of herself now."**
- **"I long for those simple days before the IRS started paying attention to me."**

*I always wanted to be somebody, but now I
realize I should have been more specific.*
— Lily Tomlin

We've all imagined it. We're in the swanky ballroom with the sparkling crystal chandeliers and velvet seats, standing at the podium, holding our gold statuette. We're looking fabulous, of course. Our hair is perfectly coiffed. We look ten years younger and have lost those extra five (*ahem*) pounds. We flash a gleaming white smile and look out at the tuxedoed and evening-gowned audience, clapping and cheering. We recognize a few familiar faces beaming back at us — those who've helped and encouraged us along the way. And way back in the corner, biting his nails, is the guy who said we'd never make it. Nah, scratch that. He's watching it at home. Alone. In the dark. Eating a Hot Pocket. Anyway, we lean toward the microphone. The room quiets down, and we begin our speech. "I'd like to thank…"

Before we writers even have our stories outlined, we've already thought about that Oscar acceptance speech. And why shouldn't we? We work *hard*. We put years into a project and often receive very little response to it, let alone accolades. We want to be respected and valued. We want our work to mean something. And besides, isn't that what awards in this business are about? Marking someone's achievement and success?

But then we read the headlines: That gorgeous actor couple who divorced after she won the Oscar and he didn't. That writer who was never again produced after winning "Best Screenplay." The producer's productions that forevermore flopped.

We never consider that those things could happen to us. We know this is a fickle business, yet we still hang our hopes on the possibility that we might be the exception. We hang on to our "if only…" hopes and dreams like amulets that ward off the bad-luck vampires.

Many people chase their dreams of success only to find out when they've "made it" that it doesn't really mean anything. They still have to slog through breaking the next story. They still have to put words on a blank screen. They still have to deal with lame notes and difficult people. And yes, while they might have some new doors opened, the most "successful" writers still struggle to see their stories produced. Even worse, their "success" has not necessarily made them happier, smarter, prettier, or thinner like they'd hoped. Success in the business is especially empty if one isn't a success in life.

Have you ever caught yourself saying any of the following?

If only I had…
> More time to write
> More money
> A better job
> No day job
> A producer

[A] supportive spouse / parents / mentors
The right connections
An agent / manager

I would be...
Happy
Fulfilled
Focused
Creative
Confident
Successful
Productive
Produced
Accomplished

These columns can never be equal to one another because they are unrelated. Circumstances don't necessarily determine one's sense of well-being.

Success is a perception, supported by validation. If someone thinks you're successful, but you don't see yourself that way, are you successful? Conversely, if you think of yourself as successful but no one else recognizes you that way, *are* you successful? What if everyone thinks you're a failure, including yourself, and you die with a drawer full of pages that someone later stumbles on, deems brilliant, and you go down in history as a "successful" writer?

So when do you know you have it? The answer is a deeply personal one. There are many layers to this question. Success is a series of goals met while in union with one's purpose in life. It is validated by the people in your life who matter to you. You can't succeed unless you have a purpose, and are in relationships with other people which give that purpose meaning.

If your purpose is to tell stories with beautiful, thought-provoking endings, then you are a success when someone reads or watches your story and finds its denouement majestic. It doesn't really matter if the story is produced, or whether it makes money at the box office. You have achieved your purpose. Or perhaps your purpose really is to yield big box-office results. Fine, but make sure validation also comes from people who matter to you and happen to be touched by your blockbuster, not just from numbers in a studio's bank account.

The first best step in having a successful career is being successful at life. By "life," we mean the quality of your relationships with others. If you succeed at life but fail as a writer, you can still have a good and meaningful life. It can be argued that anyone who succeeds at life can never really fail at anything else. If you fail at life, it won't matter how rich, famous, or brilliant you become in your career. You'll still feel empty.

Think about your own definition of success. Make a list of milestones and goals, which could be markers of success for you. What circumstances need to occur before you deem yourself a successful writer who is also successful at life? Now go back over the list. How many of those circumstances are under your control? What are the behaviors you need to practice on a daily basis to help you reach those goals? Chances are, there are many things you can do today to help you on your path; but the ultimate outcome depends upon uncontrollable factors — time, fate, and the validation of others. However, if you are in constant possession of the things that are in your control, your odds of success are excellent.

What if you do make a name for yourself, and you find yourself suddenly rubbing elbows with the inner circles of Hollywood? It can happen. And, contrary to what you hear on *TMZ*, it is possible to acquire riches and fame and still be a kind, good, and decent person. Here are some things to keep in mind:

Remember the Little Guys

With riches and fame come people who are suddenly interested in you. They perceive your success as a means to an end, something they can use or exploit for their own advancement. These people don't actually care about who you are as a person. Similarly, we know plenty of individuals who, as they rise through the ranks, lose people they thought were friends along the way, because those "friends" become jealous of their success. If your friend can't be genuinely happy for you when something good happens, then he or she is not your friend. The people with whom you do want to align are the ones who have supported you throughout. They know you and like you regardless of your IMDB ranking. These are your lifelong friends, whose relationships you should continue to nurture.

Save and Invest Your Money

There is no such thing as steady employment as a professional screen-writer. Every project is temporary. It is extremely important to save money and live modestly, even when money is rolling in. A success-ful writer can go several years between gigs. The median salary for working, professional screenwriters, according to the WGA, is less than $30,000 per year. That means in any given year that a handful of writers are making a lot of money, while most are making zero.

This Too Shall Pass... Even Success

Even the most successful careers end sometime. Many screenwriters, if credited at all, only rack up one credit in their lifetime. Projects and deals are constantly shifting, and any professional writer may have upwards of a dozen projects which may or may not be happening at any given time. If you find yourself suddenly in great demand, which is great, know that it is only a season. Which brings us to...

Enjoy the Ride

While there are periods of hard, monotonous work, and anxiety-inducing deals, being a screenwriter can also be glorious, exciting, and fun. Our wish for every screenwriter is to have the wherewithal to enjoy those fun moments. After all, it is a privilege to be us. We work with some of the most creative minds of our generation. We get to create whole worlds out of our imagination. Sometimes, our work touches people's lives. And sure, while there are many stressors in our line of work, we get to do something that not many people get to do. Enjoy it.

CHAPTER 26

FAQS ABOUT THE BUSINESS

The following are the questions we are most commonly asked.

I know there's a whole chapter on working with producers... but I still want to know how to get an agent.

In our experience, you don't get an agent. An agent gets you. That is, after you have broken in and are making money, an agent will suddenly appear in your doorway wanting to help you move your career to the next level.

Cream rises to the top. Agents know that, and they also know that a writer who has made it past the beginning is probably a better bet for the long haul. Contrary to what most beginning writers think, agents are not interested in projects as much as they are interested in writers. They want people from whom they can make a lot of money for many years. They are looking for real signs of commitment and skill in this profession.

It can help a writer get noticed by an agent if the writer wins a screenwriting contest, or their web series goes viral, or they write something low budget that gets rave reviews. In terms of projects, agents are looking for something they can sell *right now*, so be ready with several samples polished and ready to go.

We know you don't believe us, but the best-case scenario is that an agent contacts you first. Many writers are referred by other working, successful people in the business; but keep in mind, you need to be so good at the craft that you are doing *them* a favor by being someone they can recommend, and not the other way around.

What's the difference between an agent, manager, and attorney?

An agent negotiates contracts on your behalf, and takes up to 15% of what you earn. A manager negotiates in the absence of an agent, but ideally offers more direction in support of your career. And they take up to 20% of what you earn. An attorney looks at your contract and advises whether it's in your best interests. And they take up to 10% of what you earn.

Make sure the attorney you hire specializes in entertainment law. On some early projects, you may end up paying your attorney more than you received! It's worth it.

While all of these professionals can assist you, it is still primarily up to the writer to find his or her own work. This is always dismaying to writers who think that they can sit back and wait for jobs to roll in once they've procured an agent or a manager.

No one will consider your career as high-stakes as you do. Agents and managers might send scripts out on your behalf and line up meet and greets, but most writers with agents and managers still bring in their own work.

Which comes first? Agent, manager, or attorney?

In most cases, an attorney comes first because most people have already written something that requires a contract before they get an agent's or manager's attention. It doesn't really matter whether you attract a manager or an agent first. Having one will help you get the other.

Do I really need all those people?

If you are a working professional making Writers Guild level deals, yes. If you are just starting out, having an attorney is the most important thing. Do not sign anything without an attorney. No matter how many times the producer sniffs that it is a bad sign that you are so untrusting. No matter how much of a friend the producer is. Especially if they're a friend! You've been warned.

What's the WGA and how do I get in?

The Writers Guild of America has East and West chapters, and is the union for working screenwriters. Writers in the union can only work with WGA signatory producers. Serious producers are Guild signatories because studio distribution and credits fall under the WGA's purview. Writers in the WGA are guaranteed minimum amounts of compensation for their work according to the Basic Agreement that was negotiated by the union. But most projects are negotiated to a higher amount to account for agent and attorney fees and whatever fee a writer can command. Writers get into the WGA by working on a signatory project. All writers, regardless of whether they are members or not, should register their work with the WGA. More information and the schedule of minimums can be found online at *www.wga.org.*

When should I get into the WGA?

When it means that you won't lose good, paying work with non-WGA signatories. When you need the health-insurance benefits and know you will make enough in subsequent years to get them (about $35,000 per year). When it is the next good step for you.

Is there any chance someone will steal my story ideas?

Yes, but it's not as likely as people outside the business tend to think. Writers should do their own due diligence to protect their screenplays and treatments. Copyrights and WGA registration and a nice long paper trail of all the previous drafts are parts of the profession, and no one will do them for you.

Ironically, we get this question the most from the writers and producers with the most sloppy, ill-conceived, and unmarketable projects. These are the folks who miss all the irony when we say, "This idea is *particularly* safe."

Should I worry about losing my credit?

It happens quite often that if a newbie screenwriter who is not in the Guild sells a script, and the project gets picked up by a WGA signatory, the writer will be "rewritten" out of their credit. And the WGA will let it happen because the union does not fight for the authorship rights of non-WGA members.

One way to make the eventual fight more interesting is to have a clause in your contract that reads something akin to: "If this project ever becomes a WGA signatory project, then the writer will be grandfathered into the WGA and be credited as the original story and screenplay writer. The production company will pay all fees and dues in support of that. Further, the writer's fee on the project will be adjusted to $_____ in recognition of WGA minimums."

I'm making my first deal. What's considered "fair"?

There are a number of factors to consider when making a deal; and again, it's always best to consult an attorney. Most first deals mean the producer is getting the writer very, very cheap. In return, the writer needs to evaluate the potential opportunity. Is the project actually going somewhere? Does it have viable distribution? Is there potential for more (better-paid) work down the road? Many producers will try to lure new writers with back-end deals, but these rarely, if ever, pay off. The best deal is to get some money, any money, up front, with some promise of a back end, should the project become wildly, unexpectedly lucrative. A writer's total fee, though negotiable, is generally between 2% and 4% of the overall budget.

Is it ever okay to work for free?

As a matter of principle, no. But you can start out working for very, very little. In fact, more likely than not, much of your first work will be nearly for free as your first jobs are not about making money but about securing happy collaborators who will say good things about you to other potential collaborators. People tend not to respect or value what they get for free. Even a token investment in you as a writer will make people treat you with a more serious disposition.

Also, producers who have sunk money into a project tend to be more urgent about marketing it.

Eventually, there comes a point in one's career where one ought to be paid appropriately. Screenwriting, and the story-development process, tend to be grossly undervalued, even though a proper investment in the process saves millions in the long run.

You say the spec market is dead. What's a spec, and do I still need to write one?

Yes. A spec script is something that you write on your own time, for free, that is a sample of your voice and talent as a writer. It is possible, but very unlikely, that a spec script will be bought and produced as a feature. It is even more unlikely that a spec for television will be bought and produced. Specs are more often used as writing samples for projects for hire. Say a producer is making an action thriller. He wants to read your spec to see how you might approach the genre or the characters he has in mind for his own story. Some producers might hire you to write their idea "on spec" (a/k/a "for no upfront pay") and then decide if they want to purchase it. This scenario happens more often than writers might like.

What about screenplay contests and festivals? Are they worth it?

Depends on the festival. Lots of festivals are being launched every year in far-flung places by people who have little or no experience as writers and producers, and absolutely no idea of the industry as a marketplace. They do it to make money off the screenplay submission fees, and mainly just because they like movies. Beware the issue contests that amount to a group of people saying, "Hey, we like fluffy bunnies. Let's have a fluffy-bunny screenplay contest to promote the awareness of cute, fluffy bunnies." That's nice, but it has nothing to do with the global marketplace. If you win the Fluffy Bunny Screenplay contest, don't expect Hollywood to be impressed.

In the end, few of the festivals are worth the price of entry to the writer. Seek out the ones that are. Send your scripts to the midlevel events that have been around for a while and offer real compensation to the contest winners. Once you get very good at your craft, you should be throwing your hat into the ring for the festivals that do mean something in the business, like the Nicholl Fellowship or the Final Draft, Inc. Big Break Contest. If you win or place as a finalist, it can be a good way to get noticed. But so many people enter these contests that the odds of winning, even when you are a spectacular writer, are minuscule. You have better odds just finding a producer on your own.

Still, it feels good to win some kind of award, even if it costs you $60, so we recommend that writers submit their work to at least three or four of these events each year. A search on *www.withoutabox. com* will pull up hundreds of script contests open at any given time.

What are some other ways of getting my script out there?

Always strive to build relationships, meet more people in the business, and work on being a generally likeable, good person. Heed the words of the wise sage, Steve Martin: *Be so good they can't ignore you.* If you're *that* good, you will get noticed. Also, hedge your bets. Start on the next project right away. Professional writers have upwards of a dozen projects in various stages at any given time. Most professionals are fortunate if even one of them pays off. For every project that makes it to the screen, there are hundreds that died in its wake. Just keep going.

CHAPTER 27

SECTION SUMMARY:
RULES FOR PROFESSIONAL SCREENWRITERS

These are some first principles we have worked out for the new writers with whom we work. They represent the collective wisdom of more than thirty years' experience as professional writers and executives. Some of them require a bit of experience to fully comprehend, and will become clearer as you move ahead in the business.

You've been warned!

Rule #1
Never make your own deals.
(You are a sheep among wolves.)

Rule #2
Never talk to producers about money.
(You will hamstring your representatives.)

Rule #3
Register your script with the WGA before you turn it over.
(But know that the registration is meaningless legally.)

Rule #4
Let your agent, manager, or attorney be the heavy.
(As far as everyone is concerned, you are a business illiterate.)

Rule #5
An agent is no substitute for a brain.
(Do not be business illiterate.)

Rule #6
Don't whine.
(It's a tough business. Sue if you must, or shut up.)

Rule #7
If you must whine, only do it to your agent or manager.
(Never to the producer, or co-producer, or main project investor, or the grip, or line producer, or craft-services person, or...)

Rule #8
Don't say anything about anybody on the project who isn't in the room listening to you.
(These are not your family or friends, they are business associates; harmony on a project means more than you do.)

Rule #9
Don't spend it until the check has cleared.
(Checks bounce more in Hollywood than any other place.)

Rule #10
Don't spend it until you have paid the IRS.
(It's always tax time for an independent contractor.)

Rule #11
Don't miss deadlines.
(To your face, they will say it's okay. Behind your back, they are saying other things.)

Rule #12
It's better to miss a deadline than to turn in a bad script.
(Be talking to your producers all through the project so they know how things are going. Find a way to get their approval if you need more time.)

Rule #13
Stay at the table as long as you can.
(Take a little less money in exchange for a creative consultant or some kind of producer credit. If you are in the room, you can fight for your script.)

Rule #14
Never believe your own hype.
(You will be "brilliant" today and "a disappointment" tomorrow. It means nothing.)

Rule #15
Cheaters cheat. Liars lie.
(Once people have breached their own internal ethics, they don't stop.)

Rule #16
Be tangibly grateful.
(Send thank-you cards, flowers, and make referrals. People remember.)

APPENDIX A

THE 100 MOST INFLUENTIAL MOVIES EVER MADE

(compiled from several lists)

1. *Intolerance* (1916)
2. *Nosferatu* (1922)
3. *Battleship Potemkin* (1925)
4. *The Gold Rush* (1925)
5. *The General* (1926)
6. *The Jazz Singer* (1927)
7. *Metropolis* (1927)
8. *Sunrise* (1927)
9. *The Passion of Joan of Arc* (1928)
10. *All Quiet on the Western Front* (1930)
11. *City Lights* (1931)
12. *M* (1931)
13. *Duck Soup* (1933)
14. *King Kong* (1933)
15. *It Happened One Night* (1934)
16. *Top Hat* (1935)
17. *Modern Times* (1936)
18. *The Grand Illusion* (1937)
19. *Snow White and the Seven Dwarfs* (1937)
20. *The Adventures of Robin Hood* (1938)
21. *Gone With the Wind* (1939)
22. *Mr. Smith Goes to Washington* (1939)
23. *Stagecoach* (1939)
24. *The Wizard of Oz* (1939)
25. *The Bank Dick* (1940)
26. *His Girl Friday* (1940)
27. *Citizen Kane* (1941)
28. *The Maltese Falcon* (1941)
29. *Casablanca* (1942)
30. *Double Indemnity* (1944)
31. *Rome, Open City* (1945)
32. *It's a Wonderful Life* (1946)
33. *The Bicycle Thief* (1948)
34. *All About Eve* (1950)
35. *Rashomon* (1950)
36. *Sunset Boulevard* (1950)
37. *The African Queen* (1951)
38. *High Noon* (1952)
39. *Ikiru* (1952)

40. *On the Waterfront* (1954)
41. *Rear Window* (1954)
42. *The Searchers* (1956)
43. *The Bridge on the River Kwai* (1957)
44. *The Seventh Seal* (1957)
45. *Vertigo* (1958)
46. *The 400 Blows* (1959)
47. *Some Like It Hot* (1959)
48. *The Apartment* (1960)
49. *Breathless* (1960)
50. *La Dolce Vita* (1960)
51. *Psycho* (1960)
52. *West Side Story* (1961)
53. *Lawrence of Arabia* (1962)
54. *The Manchurian Candidate* (1962)
55. *To Kill a Mockingbird* (1962)
56. *8½* (1963)
57. *The Great Escape* (1963)
58. *Dr. Strangelove* (1964)
59. *The Gospel According to St. Matthew* (1964)
60. *Andrei Rublev* (1966)
61. *A Man for All Seasons* (1966)
62. *Belle de Jour* (1967)
63. *Bonnie and Clyde* (1967)
64. *2001: A Space Odyssey* (1968)
65. *Butch Cassidy and the Sundance Kid* (1969)
66. *The Wild Bunch* (1969)
67. *The Godfather* (1972)
68. *Chinatown* (1974)
69. *The Godfather: Part II* (1974)

70. *Jaws* (1975)
71. *Taxi Driver* (1976)
72. *Annie Hall* (1977)
73. *Star Wars* (1977)
74. *Apocalypse Now* (1979)
75. *The Elephant Man* (1980)
76. *Raiders of the Lost Ark* (1981)
77. *Blade Runner* (1982)
78. *E.T. the Extra-Terrestrial* (1982)
79. *This Is Spinal Tap* (1984)
80. *Back to the Future* (1985)
81. *Babette's Feast* (1987)
82. *Raising Arizona* (1987)
83. *Crimes and Misdemeanors* (1989)
84. *When Harry Met Sally...* (1989)
85. *The Silence of the Lambs* (1991)
86. *Unforgiven* (1992)
87. *Groundhog Day* (1993)
88. *Pulp Fiction* (1994)
89. *Toy Story* (1995)
90. *Fargo* (1996)
91. *Titanic* (1997)
92. *Saving Private Ryan* (1998)
93. *The Truman Show* (1998)
94. *The Matrix* (1999)
95. *The Royal Tenenbaums* (2001)
96. *Spirited Away* (2001)
97. *In America* (2002)
98. *The Dark Knight* (2008)
99. *The Artist* (2011)
100. *Gravity* (2013)

APPENDIX B
CORRECTLY FORMATTED TITLE PAGE

Select Society

by
Barbara Nicolosi

Based on, If Any

Current Revision
September 2014

Represented by
Bauman Management

Barbara Nicolosi
999 My Street
Los Angeles, CA
Phone Number

CORRECTLY FORMATTED FIRST PAGE

FADE IN

INT. AMHERST COLLEGE — A LARGE PARLOR — DAY (1896)

Blinking behind spectacles, A YOUNG MAN raises his hand.

> YOUNG MAN
> Can't you tell us why? Why she
> never left her house? Why she let
> no one see her?

An audience of robed COLLEGE STUDENTS and prim Yankee
TOWNSPEOPLE sits in rows in the impressive paneled room lined
with book shelves. A large fireplace on one wall warms the
room. The people turn from looking at the student to...

MABEL LOOMIS TODD (44), who makes a pretty picture in her
hand-embroidered dress and dainty hat. But her diminutive
build and features can't mask her glint of ambition. She
flutters her hand with a practiced air.

> MABLE
> It is certainly the most pressing
> mystery of Amherst these nearly
> three decades. Perhaps of all
> literary history.

The people in the crowd nod and stare, entranced by Mabel.

> MABLE (CONT'D)
> As someone who shared a great
> intimacy with the poet, I have my
> own, well-informed opinion.

Mabel pauses to let her status sink in with the crowd.

A YOUNG GIRL chews on some gum with rapt attention.

A robed PROFESSOR looks up from the pages of a green book.

> PROFESSOR
> Dante had his Beatrice. Browning
> had his Elizabeth. So, who...?

> MABLE
> Ah, and the second great mystery!
> What was her great love story? We
> all know she must have had one.
> No one could write so much of love
> without having felt it first in her
> own heart.

The professor nods gravely.

APPENDIX D

CORRECTLY FORMATTED INTERIOR PAGE

From *Zoe and the Zebra* by Vicki Peterson

MOMENTS LATER

Zoe picks at the eggs, but her guilt won't let her eat them. A hungry raccoon watches from the safety of a nearby bush. Zoe uses a stick to knock the can off the fire, eggs sliding into the dirt. She walks off.

The raccoon gobbles the treat.

BLACKBERRY BUSHES — DAY

Zoe collects berries, popping every other one into her mouth, careful not to touch the poison oak. She hears a RUSTLE of leaves, and turns to see a peacock, with his beautiful plumage, disappear under a bush.

Zoe investigates. She wanders into the bushes, following the peacock into a canopy of-

WILLOWS

The peacock flies into a willow tree and perches there, with his tail hanging down in an arc. Zoe creeps closer and studies the beautiful bird.

Behind Zoe, something follows her.

Zoe takes a step closer and reaches a hand out to touch the plumage.

                    ZOE
          What are you doing out here?

Her voice spooks the bird. It lets out a high-pitched WAIL.

Zoe jumps back.

Zoe hears a SNUFFLE behind her and turns around as the bird flutters off.

Zoe stands eye to eye with the zebra.

Zoe freezes. She and the zebra stand there, inches from each other's faces, equally stunned.

The zebra, not yet fully grown, is about the size of a pony. Its deep, dark eyes match the wonder in Zoe's.

Zoe looks down. The zebra favors its right leg, holding its left hoof off the ground; a piece of barbed wire pierces into its skin.

The zebra nuzzles Zoe's closed hand, where she still holds some berries.

BIBLIOGRAPHY

Aristotle (translated by Malcolm Heath). *The Poetics.* Penguin Classics (1997).

Catron, Dr. Louis. *The Elements of Playwriting.* Waveland Press (2001).

McLaughlin, Buzz. *The Playwright's Process: Learning the Craft from Today's Leading Dramatists.* Back Stage Books (2011).

Man of Steel, short synopsis, from the Internet Movie Database, *www. imdb.com/title/tt0770828/plotsummary?ref_=tt_ql_6*

Movies quoted:

Casablanca (1942), Warner Bros., screenplay by Julius J. Epstein and Philip G. Epstein and Howard Koch

Conspiracy Theory (1997), Warner Bros., Silver Pictures, screenplay by Brian Helgeland

Double Indemnity (1944), Paramount Pictures, screenplay by Billy Wilder and Raymond Chandler

A Few Good Men (1992), Castle Rock Entertainment, Columbia Pictures, screenplay by Aaron Sorkin

The Fugitive (1993), Warner Bros., screenplay by Jeb Stuart and David Twohy

Glengarry Glen Ross (1992), GGR, New Line Cinema, Zupnik Cinema Group II, screenplay by David Mamet

Gone With the Wind (1939), Warner Bros., screenplay by Sidney Howard

Jerry Maguire (1996), TriStar Pictures, Gracie Films, screenplay by Cameron Crowe

Jurassic Park (1993), Universal Pictures, Amblin Entertainment, screenplay by Michael Crichton and David Koepp

A Man for All Seasons (1966), Highland Films, screenplay by Robert Bolt

Patton (1970), 20th Century Fox, screenplay by Francis Ford Coppola and Edmund H. North

The Philadelphia Story (1940), Metro-Goldwyn-Mayer, screenplay by Donald Ogden Stewart

When Harry Met Sally... (1989), Castle Rock Entertainment, Nelson Entertainment, screenplay by Nora Ephron

ABOUT THE AUTHORS

A California native, **VICKI PETERSON** is a screenwriter and founding partner of Catharsis, which offers script consulting, event speaking, and development and writing services for multiple production companies. Vicki's projects include a television pilot being produced by Herrick  Entertainment, *Alum Rock Ave*; and *Mother at War*, to which Ken Stewart is attached. Her other projects include features, TV specs, and rewrites for production companies; and her scripts have won and been selected as finalists for several film festivals and fellowships.

Vicki was formerly the director of both the Writing for Film and Television program and the Producing and Entertainment Executive program at Act One, Inc. (*www.actoneprogram.com*), founded by her business partner, Barbara Nicolosi. Vicki designed curriculum and managed over 150 faculty members, including top writers and producers in the entertainment industry. She also mentored and supported a community of over 700 alumni, many of whom have gone on to very successful careers in the industry. Before that, Vicki was a development executive at Origin Entertainment and Hero Pictures, and also worked at the management company Industry Entertainment. Vicki got her start in theater, working at the Tony Award–winning La Jolla Playhouse on several Broadway-bound productions. Vicki has BA in theater from the University of California, San Diego, and is an alumna of Act One. She is an MFA candidate in Writing for Stage and Screen at the New Hampshire Institute of Art, and has been a guest lecturer at many colleges and universities.

Originally from Portsmouth, Rhode Island, **BARBARA NICOLOSI** is the Founder and Chair Emeritus of Act One, Inc., a non-profit program to train and mentor young people for careers as Hollywood writers and executives. She is a founding partner of Catharsis, and has worked as a develop-ment executive at Paulist Productions in Malibu, California, and Origin Entertainment in Manhattan Beach, California. Barbara has been an adjunct professor at Pepperdine University, the Los Angeles Film Study Center, and Azusa Pacific University.

Barbara is a member of the Writers Guild of America, West, and has written screenplays for several Hollywood production companies. Her most recent credit is as a writer on the 2015 Lionsgate release *Mary*. In addition to producing several award-winning plays at the Actors Co-op Theatres in Hollywood, Barbara executive-produced the 2010 Origin Entertainment 3D documentary *Cosmic Origins*, and the short film *In Memory* (2014). Barbara has consulted on hundreds of scripts and projects, including the movie *The Passion of the Christ* and the television shows *Judging Amy* and *Saving Grace*.

A multiple award–winning magazine columnist, Barbara was also coeditor of the 2006 Baker Books title *Behind the Screen: Hollywood Insiders on Faith, Film, and Culture*. She blogs at churchofthemasses. blogspot.com.

THE MYTH OF MWP

In a dark time, a light bringer came along, leading the curious and the frustrated to clarity and empowerment. It took the well-guarded secrets out of the hands of the few and made them available to all. It spread a spirit of openness and creative freedom, and built a storehouse of knowledge dedicated to the betterment of the arts.

The essence of the Michael Wiese Productions (MWP) is empowering people who have the burning desire to express themselves creatively. We help them realize their dreams by putting the tools in their hands. We demystify the sometimes secretive worlds of screenwriting, directing, acting, producing, film financing, and other media crafts.

By doing so, we hope to bring forth a realization of 'conscious media' which we define as being positively charged, emphasizing hope and affirming positive values like trust, cooperation, self-empowerment, freedom, and love. Grounded in the deep roots of myth, it aims to be healing both for those who make the art and those who encounter it. It hopes to be transformative for people, opening doors to new possibilities and pulling back veils to reveal hidden worlds.

MWP has built a storehouse of knowledge unequaled in the world, for no other publisher has so many titles on the media arts. Please visit www.mwp.com where you will find many free resources and a 25% discount on our books. Sign up and become part of the wider creative community!

Onward and upward,

Michael Wiese
Publisher/Filmmaker